LLEWELLYN'S 2022

Sabbats
ALMANAC

Samhain 2021
to
Mabon 2022

Llewellyn's 2022 Sabbats Almanac
Samhain 2021 to Mabon 2022

Cover art © Carolyn Vibbert
Cover design by Shira Atakpu
Editing by Hanna Grimson
Interior Art: © Carolyn Vibbert, excluding illustrations on pages 34, 70, 109, 146, 185, 221, 256, 294, which are © Wen Hsu

You can order annuals and books from *New Worlds*, Llewellyn's catalog. To request a free copy, call 1-877-NEW WRLD toll-free or order online by visiting our website at http://subscriptions.llewellyn.com.

ISBN: 978-0-7387-6050-6

Llewellyn Worldwide Ltd.
2143 Wooddale Drive
Woodbury, MN 55125-2989
www.llewellyn.com

Printed in the United States of America

Contents

2021

JANUARY
S	M	T	W	T	F	S
					1	2
3	4	5	6	7	8	9
10	11	12	13	14	15	16
17	18	19	20	21	22	23
24	25	26	27	28	29	30
31						

FEBRUARY
S	M	T	W	T	F	S
	1	2	3	4	5	6
7	8	9	10	11	12	13
14	15	16	17	18	19	20
21	22	23	24	25	26	27
28						

MARCH
S	M	T	W	T	F	S
	1	2	3	4	5	6
7	8	9	10	11	12	13
14	15	16	17	18	19	20
21	22	23	24	25	26	27
28	29	30	31			

APRIL
S	M	T	W	T	F	S
				1	2	3
4	5	6	7	8	9	10
11	12	13	14	15	16	17
18	19	20	21	22	23	24
25	26	27	28	29	30	

MAY
S	M	T	W	T	F	S
						1
2	3	4	5	6	7	8
9	10	11	12	13	14	15
16	17	18	19	20	21	22
23	24	25	26	27	28	29
30	31					

JUNE
S	M	T	W	T	F	S
		1	2	3	4	5
6	7	8	9	10	11	12
13	14	15	16	17	18	19
20	21	22	23	24	25	26
27	28	29	30			

JULY
S	M	T	W	T	F	S
				1	2	3
4	5	6	7	8	9	10
11	12	13	14	15	16	17
18	19	20	21	22	23	24
25	26	27	28	29	30	31

AUGUST
S	M	T	W	T	F	S
1	2	3	4	5	6	7
8	9	10	11	12	13	14
15	16	17	18	19	20	21
22	23	24	25	26	27	28
29	30	31				

SEPTEMBER
S	M	T	W	T	F	S
			1	2	3	4
5	6	7	8	9	10	11
12	13	14	15	16	17	18
19	20	21	22	23	24	25
26	27	28	29	30		

OCTOBER
S	M	T	W	T	F	S
					1	2
3	4	5	6	7	8	9
10	11	12	13	14	15	16
17	18	19	20	21	22	23
24	25	26	27	28	29	30
31						

NOVEMBER
S	M	T	W	T	F	S
	1	2	3	4	5	6
7	8	9	10	11	12	13
14	15	16	17	18	19	20
21	22	23	24	25	26	27
28	29	30				

DECEMBER
S	M	T	W	T	F	S
			1	2	3	4
5	6	7	8	9	10	11
12	13	14	15	16	17	18
19	20	21	22	23	24	25
26	27	28	29	30	31	

2022

JANUARY
S	M	T	W	T	F	S
						1
2	3	4	5	6	7	8
9	10	11	12	13	14	15
16	17	18	19	20	21	22
23	24	25	26	27	28	29
30	31					

FEBRUARY
S	M	T	W	T	F	S
		1	2	3	4	5
6	7	8	9	10	11	12
13	14	15	16	17	18	19
20	21	22	23	24	25	26
27	28					

MARCH
S	M	T	W	T	F	S
		1	2	3	4	5
6	7	8	9	10	11	12
13	14	15	16	17	18	19
20	21	22	23	24	25	26
27	28	29	30	31		

APRIL
S	M	T	W	T	F	S
					1	2
3	4	5	6	7	8	9
10	11	12	13	14	15	16
17	18	19	20	21	22	23
24	25	26	27	28	29	30

MAY
S	M	T	W	T	F	S
1	2	3	4	5	6	7
8	9	10	11	12	13	14
15	16	17	18	19	20	21
22	23	24	25	26	27	28
29	30	31				

JUNE
S	M	T	W	T	F	S
			1	2	3	4
5	6	7	8	9	10	11
12	13	14	15	16	17	18
19	20	21	22	23	24	25
26	27	28	29	30		

JULY
S	M	T	W	T	F	S
					1	2
3	4	5	6	7	8	9
10	11	12	13	14	15	16
17	18	19	20	21	22	23
24	25	26	27	28	29	30
31						

AUGUST
S	M	T	W	T	F	S
	1	2	3	4	5	6
7	8	9	10	11	12	13
14	15	16	17	18	19	20
21	22	23	24	25	26	27
28	29	30	31			

SEPTEMBER
S	M	T	W	T	F	S
				1	2	3
4	5	6	7	8	9	10
11	12	13	14	15	16	17
18	19	20	21	22	23	24
25	26	27	28	29	30	

OCTOBER
S	M	T	W	T	F	S
						1
2	3	4	5	6	7	8
9	10	11	12	13	14	15
16	17	18	19	20	21	22
23	24	25	26	27	28	29
30	31					

NOVEMBER
S	M	T	W	T	F	S
		1	2	3	4	5
6	7	8	9	10	11	12
13	14	15	16	17	18	19
20	21	22	23	24	25	26
27	28	29	30			

DECEMBER
S	M	T	W	T	F	S
				1	2	3
4	5	6	7	8	9	10
11	12	13	14	15	16	17
18	19	20	21	22	23	24
25	26	27	28	29	30	31

Ostara

Beltane

Litha

Lammas

Contents

Mabon

Introduction

NEARLY EVERYONE HAS A favorite sabbat. There are numerous ways to observe any tradition. The 2022 edition of the *Sabbats Almanac* provides a wealth of lore, celebrations, creative projects, and recipes to enhance your holiday.

For this edition, a mix of writers—Lupa, Kate Freuler, Laura Tempest Zakroff, Ivo Dominguez Jr., Blake Octavian Blair, and more—share their ideas and wisdom. These include a variety of paths as well as the authors' personal approaches to each sabbat. Each chapter closes with an extended ritual, which may be adapted for both solitary practitioners and covens.

In addition to these insights and rituals, specialists in astrology, history, cooking, crafts, and spells impart their expertise throughout.

Robin Ivy Payton gives an overview of planetary influences most relevant for each sabbat season and provides details about the New and Full Moons, retrograde motion, planetary positions, and more.

Jason Mankey explores history, myths, and practices from around the world and how they connect to and sometimes influence each sabbat. From Maman Brigitte to the Eleusian Mysteries, this section is the place for celebration.

Elizabeth Barrette conjures up a feast for each festival that features seasonal appetizers, entrées, desserts, and beverages.

Charlie Rainbow Wolf offers instructions on DIY crafts that will help you tap into each sabbats' energy and fill your home with magic and fun.

Ember Grant provides candle magic tips and spells to celebrate and utilize the unique forces in each season.

About the Authors

Blake Octavian Blair is a shamanic and druidic practitioner, ordained minister, writer, Usui Reiki Master-Teacher, tarot reader, and musical artist. Blake incorporates mystical traditions from both the East and West with a reverence for the natural world into his own brand of spirituality. Blake holds a degree in English and religion from the University of Florida. He is an avid reader, knitter, crafter, and member of the Order of Bards, Ovates, and Druids (OBOD). He loves communing with nature and exploring its beauty whether it is within the city or hiking in the woods. Blake lives in the New England region of the US with his beloved husband. Visit him on the web at www.blakeoctavianblair.com.

Kate Freuler lives in Ontario, Canada, and is the author of *Of Blood and Bones: Working with Shadow Magick & the Dark Moon*. She has owned and operated the witchcraft shop www.whitemoon witchcraft.com for ten years. When she's not writing or crafting items for clients, she is busy being creative with art or reading a huge stack of books.

Ember Grant is the author of *Magical Candle Crafting*, *The Book of Crystal Spells*, and *The Second Book of Crystal Spells*, and she has been contributing to Llewellyn's annuals series since 2003. She lives in Missouri with her husband and two feline companions.

Jason Mankey is a Wiccan-Witch who lives in Northern California with his wife, Ari, and two cats. He's the author of *Transformative Witchcraft: The Greater Mysteries*, *Witch's Wheel of the Year: Rituals for Circles, Solitaries & Covens*, and several books in the Witch's Tools series. He writes online at the blog *Raise the Horns*.

Suzanne Ress has been practicing Wicca for about twelve years as the leader of a small coven, but she has been aware of having a special connection to nature and animal spirits since she was a young child. She has been writing creatively most of her life—short stories, novels, and nonfiction articles for a variety of publications—and finds it to be an important outlet for her considerable creative powers. Other outlets she regularly makes use of are metalsmithing, mosaic works, painting, and all kinds of dance. She is also a professional aromatic herb grower and beekeeper. Although she is an American of Welsh ancestry by birth, she has lived in northern Italy for nearly twenty years. She recently discovered that the small mountain in the pre-alpine hills that she inhabits with her family and animals was once the site of an ancient Insubrian Celtic sacred place. Not surprisingly, the top of the mountain has remained a fulcrum of sacredness throughout the millennia, and this grounding in blessedness makes Suzanne's everyday life especially magical.

Charlie Rainbow Wolf is happiest when she is creating something, especially if it's made from items that others have discarded. Pottery, writing, knitting, astrology, and tarot ignite her passion, but she happily confesses she's easily distracted; life offers such wonderful things to explore! A recorded singer-songwriter and published author, she champions holistic living and lives in the Midwest with her husband and special needs Great Danes. Visit her at www.charlierainbow.com.

Laura Tempest Zakroff is a professional artist, author, dancer, designer, and Modern Traditional Witch based in New England. She holds a BFA from RISD (Rhode Island School of Design) and her artwork has received awards and honors worldwide. Her work embodies myth and the esoteric through her drawings and paintings, jewelry, talismans, and other designs. Laura is the author of the best-selling Llewellyn books *Weave the Liminal* and *Sigil Witchery*, as well as *Anatomy of a Witch, Liminal Spirits Oracle* (artist/author), *The Witch's Cauldron*, and the coauthor of *The Witch's*

Altar with Jason Mankey. Laura edited *The New Aradia: A Witch's Handbook to Magical Resistance* (Revelore Press). She blogs for Patheos as A Modern Traditional Witch, Witches & Pagans as Fine Art Witchery, and contributes to *The Witches' Almanac, Ltd*. She is the creative force behind several community events and teaches workshops worldwide. Visit her at www.LauraTempestZakroff.com.

Tess Whitehurst is a co-host of the *Magic Monday* podcast as well as the founder and facilitator of the Good Vibe Tribe Online School of Magical Arts. She has written nine books that have been translated into eighteen languages, including *Unicorn Magic: Awaken to Mystical Energy & Embrace Your Personal Power*. She's also the author of the *Magic of Flowers Oracle* and *The Cosmic Dancer Oracle*. She lives in the Rocky Mountains of Colorado.

Ivo Dominguez Jr. has been active in Wicca and the Pagan community since 1978. He is an Elder of the Assembly of the Sacred Wheel, a Wiccan syncretic tradition, and is one of its founders. He is a part of the core group that started and manages the New Alexandrian Library. Ivo is the author of *The Four Elements of the Wise: Working with the Magickal Powers of Earth, Air, Water, Fire, Keys to Perception, Practical Astrology for Witches and Pagans, Casting Sacred Space, Spirit Speak, Beneath the Skins*, and numerous shorter works. Ivo is also a professional astrologer who has studied astrology since 1980 and has been offering consultations and readings since 1988. Visit him at www.ivodominguezjr.com.

Robin Ivy Payton teaches yoga and trains yoga teachers in the Portland, Maine area. She created Robin's Zodiac Zone daily forecasts for print and broadcast in 1999 and has been writing for Llewellyn publications since 2003. A lifelong student and practitioner of the intuitive arts, Robin offers readings, teaches tarot, and guides yoga nidra journeys. Inspired by nature, she lives close to the ocean with her husband and dogs. Find or contact her through *Robin's Zodiac Zone* blog.

Lupa is a naturalist Pagan who has been exploring the wild places of the Pacific Northwest since 2006. She is the author of several books on nature-based Paganism and vulture culture, and is also the creator of the Tarot of Bones. She creates a wide variety of art with hides, bones, and other natural materials. She may be found online at http://www.thegreenwolf.com.

Elizabeth Barrette has been involved with the Pagan community for more than thirty-one years. She served as managing editor of *PanGaia* for eight years and dean of studies at the Grey School of Wizardry for four years. She has written columns on beginning and intermediate Pagan practice, Pagan culture, and Pagan leadership. Her book *Composing Magic: How to Create Magical Spells, Rituals, Blessings, Chants, and Prayers* explains how to combine writing and spirituality. She lives in central Illinois where she has done much networking with Pagans in her area, such as coffeehouse meetings and open sabbats. Her other public activities feature Pagan picnics and science fiction conventions. She enjoys magical crafts, historic religions, and gardening for wildlife. Her other writing fields include speculative fiction, gender studies, and social and environmental issues. Visit her blog *The Wordsmith's Forge* (https://ysabetwordsmith.dreamwidth.org/) or website PenUltimate Productions (http://penultimateproductions.weebly.com). Her coven site with extensive Pagan materials is Greenhaven Tradition (http://greenhaventradition.weebly.com/).

Natalie Zaman is the author of the award-winning books *Color and Conjure* (with Wendy Martin) and *Magical Destinations of the Northeast* and is a regular contributor to various Llewellyn annual publications. Visit Natalie online at http://nataliezaman.blogspot.com.

Samhain

A Drollish Samhain

Natalie Zaman

IT MAY BE A bit odd to think of Samhain in the springtime, but every turning of the wheel encompasses bits of the sabbats that proceed and follow it. You can sense Samhain's shadows in the corner of a sunny day, the rustle in the underbrush that is heard but not seen. And, perhaps, in a flock of flying pigs. Or dogs that play musical instruments. Or an army of angry—and armed—bunnies. If you've been online at all in the past year (or five), you've probably seen at least one of the articles that gets a resurgence in popularity when the world is ready for daffodils and colored eggs. My personal favorite is "Drolleries of the Middle Ages Included Comical Yet Sinister Killer Rabbits and Erotic Art" by Wu Mingren (Mingren 2019). It's a brief study of rabbits (and other creatures) making mischief in the margins of medieval manuscripts. Welcome to the world of the drollery—where even if it's spring or summer, Samhain is in the air.

Pigs with Wings and Stranger Things

I love how animals are depicted in medieval art, the "normal" and the not so normal. Drolleries are far from normal. My first encounter with them was in the Sean Connery film *The Name of the Rose*. Set in a fourteenth-century Benedictine monastery famed for its scriptorium, Connery's character, Friar William, comes to attend a debate but ends up sleuthing when the monks start dying under increasingly suspect circumstances. William (who also has a thing for books) visits the scriptorium to examine a manuscript that was being worked on by one of the victims. The young monk's unusual illustrations are fascinating: a donkey reading the scriptures to a group of bishops, the Pope as a fox, and the abbot as a monkey. Was this a statement of the state of the church at the time? Or a commentary on the small monastic community in which the artist lived—or perhaps a bit of both?

These subtle additions are typical drollery fare, providing the reader with a bit of levity in what was probably some hefty reading. Drolleries, also called grotesques (no surprise that they fall into the same category as gargoyles) are whimsical and often comic illustrations that appear in the margins (and are sometimes hidden in the details of larger illustrations and lettering) of devotional medieval books such as Psalters (books of Psalms) or books of hours—decorative samplers of church services for folks who wanted to incorporate a bit of the monastic into their lay lifestyles. These were luxury items made for the literate and the wealthy. Interestingly, books of hours were often made for women and given as wedding gifts. (To remind them of their role and duties including, via the drolleries, the naughty bits?)

As an art form, drolleries saw their heyday between the thirteenth and fifteenth centuries when custom devotional books drawn by hand were popular. Bestiaries, which date back to the classical world, undoubtedly influenced drollery art; both utilize the symbolism and moral lessons associated with animals and come from a time when Pagan and Christian sensibilities were not so far removed from each other as they would become.

So, if you were a literate medieval lady of rank, what would you see in the margins of your book of hours when you cracked it open to say your morning prayers? You might, perhaps, encounter animals "playing" humans: monkeys doing household chores like sweeping or churning butter or a rabbit riding a dog and "hawking"—but with a snail on its arm. The animals might be wearing clothes or armor. You may also see humans interacting with animals. Curiouser still, you might find animal, animal-human, and even animal-human-plant combinations: the head and forehooves of a deer emerging from a snail's shell, a rooster with a man's head, or a lady (shockingly naked!) with a stem and leaves sprouting from her head. Erotica was not off limits in drollery art, and while rabbits played their part in this (because, rabbits), a drollery could also take the form of a full on and sometimes explicit illustration—related to the text of course and undoubtedly placed there to illustrate behaviors in which persons of quality should not be engaged—but illustrated, in case you weren't exactly sure what that should mean.

Drolleries were comments and annotations purposefully included to illustrate the story with which they were paired while others were added later as asides and afterthoughts. Illuminators didn't limit themselves to illustrations—they were calligraphers after all. Words and scribbles also made appearances, giving rare glimpses into the lives of these often-anonymous artists and how they were feeling:

"The parchment is hairy." (Ew!)

"The ink is thin…"

"Oh, my hand." (I can relate!)

You can find these and more monkish scribblings in the Spring 2012 edition of *Lapham's Quarterly* ("Marginalized").

Examples of individual drollery creatures can be seen with a quick visit to Pinterest, but you can also view entire manuscripts, some of them annotated and transcribed for easy reading. One of the most famous, *The Croy Hours*, has so many drolleries in it that it's been nicknamed "The Book of Drolleries" and contains animals going about human business as well as human-animal hybrids, some of which are so cleverly illustrated that you can see the backside of the figures from the opposite page when you turn it over. The British Library has digitized whole and partial manuscripts with drolleries including *The Gorleston Psalter* and *The Taymouth Hours*. Both books contain illustrations, prayers, Bible stories, lives of the saints, and tales of chivalric romance—all material that is ripe for droll commentary.

While anthropomorphism has been around for a while, a drollery is different in that it has that topsy-turvy quality that gives one pause; it draws the viewer in to look closer and stop and think. I've found this spirit alive and well in the world today: in the decorative art trays by French designer ibride where animal heads are placed on classic paintings, in films like *Fantastic Mr. Fox*, and books like *The Wind in the Willows*. The word "droll" itself is telling as it denotes dry wit with a side of curiosity and strangeness. Archaically, droll refers to a buffoon or jester—in other words, the Fool. The trickster—often portrayed as an animal: the coyote. So Samhain is, perhaps, the drollest of Sabbats. It is the holy day of the trickster, for on this day more than any other, things are not as they seem.

Humans have always taken on animal guises. Even our language melds us together to describe character traits and physical features:

Porcine eyes

Chicken hearted

Fox lady

Mulish

Bearish

Boarish (and boorish!)

But when do we truly embrace our animal nature? When the shadows of October emerge from their corners to encroach upon the light, when the rustle in the undergrowth emerges from hiding, Samhain is upon us! It's time to step out of the pages of an illuminated story...and into the monster's ball!

Further Reading and Viewing

Annaud, Jean-Jaques, dir. *The Name of the Rose.* Sean Connery, Christian Slater, Helmut Qualtinger. 20th Century Fox, Warner Bros. Pictures, 1986. DVD.

Grahame, Kenneth. *The Wind in the Willows*. Sterling Illustrated Classics. New York: Sterling Children's Books, 2012.

References
"Digitised Manuscripts." British Library. Accessed August 14, 2020. http://www.bl.uk/manuscripts/.
"Marginalized: Notes in Manuscripts and Colophons made by Medieval Scribes and Copyists." *Lapham's Quarterly*. Accessed August 14, 2020. https://www.laphamsquarterly.org /communication/charts-graphs/marginalized.
Mingren, Wu. "Drolleries of the Middle Ages Included Comical Yet Sinister Killer Rabbits and Erotic Art." Ancient Origins. Stella Novus. April 6, 2019. https://www.ancient-origins.net /history-ancient-traditions/drolleries-0011705.

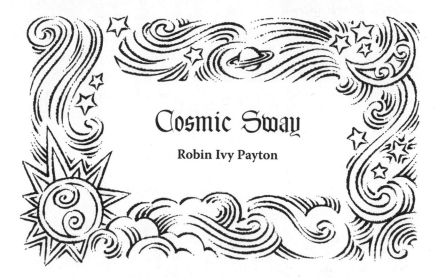

Cosmic Sway

Robin Ivy Payton

WIDELY CELEBRATED OCTOBER 31 through the first day of November, Samhain marks the cross quarter, the midpoint between the autumnal equinox and Winter Solstice.

Samhain: Summer's End

This year, the cross quarter coincides with the end of Daylight Saving Time on November 7, 2021. Samhain translates to "summer's end." In this death cycle after growth and light, some animals hibernate and the earth rests. Harvest concludes, daylight diminishes, and the colder season sets in. With garlic and bulbs now planted, farmers and gardeners make other preparations for fertility in the spring. In this liminal time between seasons, the veil between worlds feels thin, amplifying our connection to spirit. Holidays and feast days falling near this cross quarter and the increase of darkness often acknowledge death and the soul. Halloween, Día de los Muertos, and All Souls' Day traditions are rooted in respect for the dead.

Halloween

The Sun moves to Scorpio, the sign of Samhain, on October 23. The Moon is waning, with the New Moon ahead on November 4. Skies will be darkening for optimum viewing of the season's constellations when Halloween arrives on October 31. The Virgo Moon and Scorpio Sun align near dawn, synchronizing the mind with the heart. Virgo Moon helps with grounding and emotional balance during the Scorpio extremes. Clear away baggage such as grudges or conflicts in this phase of letting go. This earth sign Moon also highlights practical tasks, creating, and baking from scratch. When night falls, connect to the natural world, root your feet in the ground, and gaze at the stars. Binoculars may help zero in on the Pleiades as they reappear annually during Halloween week.

New Moon and Full Moon

November's Moons fall in sensual signs, amplifying our responses to sound, sight, scent, taste, and touch. In sacred space, perhaps somewhere outdoors, allow yourself time to breathe well, sense, and feel. With heightened awareness, notice what the Moon and all of nature has to say. Back your intentions with Scorpio passion and wisdom as the lunar cycle starts on November 4. Decisions made close to this Super New Moon are said to have long-term effects. Plan to keep promises, show loyalty, and follow through. Uranus is directly across from the Sun and Moon for unexpected feelings and eventfulness. Practice anchoring techniques such as focusing on third eye center and steadying your breath to center through shifts and intensity.

On November 19, the Moon is Full in Taurus, with a partial eclipse visible in many areas of the world. A lunar eclipse signifies rapid or unexpected conclusions. Though Taurus Moon leans toward persistence, this lunar eclipse makes letting go inevitable. Outdated roles, relationships, and financial agreements may dissolve to make space for what's ahead. Commit fully in new endeavors while releasing the past.

While the Moon peaks in this physical sign, body wisdom speaks. Full Moon symptoms can sometimes seem magnified, only to later wane. Attune to somatic, sometimes subtle, information direct from the flesh and bones. Taurus governs the neck and throat, empowering the voice. Find something to sing about as the Moon lights up. A song that arises spontaneously relieves or expresses heartfelt intention. Enhance Full Moon spells with song to invite healing, freedom from judgment, and a connection to inner power. As the Taurus Full Moon and eclipse unleashes powerful energies, open your voice and let go!

Astrology, Tarot, and Crystals

On your altar or other display, include some dark and smoky crystals known for grounding. Obsidian absorbs negativity while smoky quartz helps reduce undesirable effects of electromagnetic currents. In the spirit of Halloween and All Souls' Day, add some labradorite for ancestral wisdom and amethyst for third eye opening. At Full Moon, blue stones like kyanite, turquoise, and lapis lazuli foster clear communication and healing of the throat.

For Halloween spells or meditations, draw the Death card from your tarot. Sometimes called Transition, Death exemplifies the movement into darkness and the promise of light's return. Though darkness can cause fear or dread, it is necessary for replenishing the earth as the Wheel of the Year turns. In ourselves, there must be room for little deaths, which make space for rebirths as well.

The King and Queen of Cups cards signify qualities of the sign Scorpio. Their element is water, and emotions are their realm. In each, you may recognize yourself or others in your life. During New Moon and Sun in Scorpio, contemplate these and other cups cards for personal and relationship insights. The King and Queen cards of this suit represent traits like compassion and devotion or manipulation and neediness. They pull the emotional strings. If one resonates, use it as a symbol for your highest good through this month's shifts. For the Full Moon in Taurus, meditate on the Empress and the pentacles suit, which signify earth and abundance.

Thanksgiving

The Sun has moved on to Sagittarius by November 25, the date of Thanksgiving in the United States. Void of course 12:46 a.m. to 10:58 a.m. EST makes way for Leo Moon. Those earlier hours require more flexibility with schedules or changes of plans. After a potent, perhaps heavy, Full Moon just days ago, the Sun and Moon in fire signs welcome lightness and stimulate enthusiasm for the rest of this holiday. Mercury is close to the Sun for joyful travels and humor. Share positivity and enjoy the ones you love. This Moon sign brings out playful spirit, so plan games, recreation, and creative options for all ages. Dress or decorate with gold, solar images, and festive candles in the spirit of fire. An atmosphere of optimism begins in the heart, governed by the Leo Moon. Whatever your Thanksgiving plans, open to generosity, gratitude, gifts, and blessings with the Sun and Moon in jubilant signs.

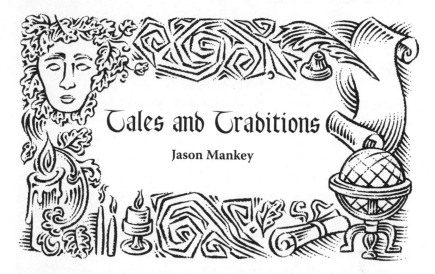

Tales and Traditions

Jason Mankey

PUMPKINS MIGHT BE THE definitive symbol of autumn. When September rolls around, "pumpkin" begins showing up nearly everywhere. It's in lattes, waffles, cereal, yogurt, and dozens of other ready-to-eat foodstuffs. In North America, pumpkin pies are routinely ranked as one of our favorite dessert pies, often only after that other mainstay, the apple pie. And at Halloween and Samhain pumpkins are virtually inescapable, the jack-o'-lantern being perhaps the most recognizable symbol of the season.

Samhain: Pumpkins & Jack-o'-Lanterns

Despite our society's obsession with pumpkins, most people know very little about them. Scientists will tell you that a "pumpkin" isn't even really a thing; what we call pumpkins today are just several different varieties of winter squash. And despite often being thought of as vegetables, squashes are fruit. Technically a pumpkin is just a very large berry! Most of the "pumpkin pie" filling we consume each year comes from winter squashes that bear very little resemblance to the orange pumpkins that sit on our porches in October.

Pumpkins are native to North America, more specifically the American South and Northeastern Mexico, and can now be found all over the world. People in Mexico began eating pumpkins nearly seven-thousand years ago! Nearly every part of a pumpkin is edible too; in addition to eating the flesh and seeds of a pumpkin, you can also eat the leaves.

Pumpkins and other winter squashes are also a part of the legendary "three sisters," which have been a staple of Native American cooking for thousands of years. Beans, corn (maize), and pumpkins or squash were all grown together in garden plots. The maize acted as poles for the beans, while the broad leaves of the pumpkin plants kept the soil moist and helped to keep out unwanted bugs and other pests (pumpkin leaves are rather prickly!). When eaten together, beans, pumpkin, and maize make for a very nutritionally complete meal.

Pumpkins are 90 percent water, making them a low-fat and healthy food (though I'm not so sure about those pumpkin spice lattes!). Pumpkins are also an excellent source of vitamins and minerals including calcium, iron, magnesium, phosphorous, and vitamins B, C, A, and E. Pumpkin oil can also help lower cholesterol. In Mexico, among certain Native American tribes, it was believed that pumpkin seeds bestowed energy and endurance upon those who ate them.

While plain old pumpkins are justifiably popular in the autumn, the pumpkin as the jack-o'-lantern symbolizes the season of Samhain for many Witches. But the exact origins of the jack-o'-lantern are difficult to pin down, and among historians there is a lot of disagreement about just how the pumpkin jack-o'-lantern came into being. Many have pointed to Ireland as the most logical place for the jack-o'-lantern's origins. According to that theory, the Irish originally carved out beets, turnips, and later potatoes and placed a small candle inside of them. The candle was to symbolize souls stuck in Catholic purgatory and perhaps offer those stuck there a way back home to their relatives.

On the surface, this theory has always made a lot of sense. In Ireland, first Samhain, and then later All Souls' Night (the evening of

November 1), have traditionally been associated with the dead, and a candle for souls stuck in purgatory has always felt appropriate. But for years there was very little evidence for the turnip-o'-lantern. Surprisingly, descriptions of lanterns made from turnips or beets are mostly absent from folklore. (They are also quite difficult to carve!) However, a turnip lantern dating from the nineteenth century was recently found in Ireland, giving more credence to this particular interpretation.

The term jack-o'-lantern probably comes from the trickster figure "Jack" who shows up in a variety of British and Irish folktales. Jack was said to be such a naughty fellow that upon his death he was denied entrance into both heaven and hell. However, the devil took pity on Jack and threw an ember from the fires of hell toward Jack, which the trickster caught in a hollowed-out turnip. From then on Jack was cursed to wander the earth until the Christian Judgement Day. This version of Jack became known as Jack-o'-lantern (Jack of the Lantern) and sometimes Stingy Jack.

The first recorded use of the term Jack-with-the-Lantern is in the *Oxford English Dictionary* from 1663, and it next shows up in 1704 in a reference to "Jack of lanthorns" (Skal 2002, 31). Both early uses of Jack-with-Lanterns were in reference to a night watchman, though our modern pumpkin-derived jack-o'-lanterns are certainly similar to watchpersons. Jack with the Lantern was often blamed for a variety of strange lights in both the British Isles and North America. Generally, these lights were the result of swamp or bog gas that looked like ghosts or lantern light in the dead of night.

Many holidays over the centuries have been associated with petty vandalism and the playing of tricks or pranks, most notably All Hallows' Eve and the Yuletide season. By the early 1800s, the term jack-o'-lantern began to be associated with pranks, though not necessarily pranks at Halloween, or any involving pumpkins. It's possible that pumpkins and jack-o'-lanterns came together in the nineteenth century as a result of Washington Irving's *The Legend of Sleepy Hollow*, which was first published in 1819.

Halloween is never mentioned in Irving's novella, but the public imagination has generally imagined the story as happening at the end of October. Jack-o'-lanterns aren't mentioned either, but the Headless Horseman does throw his head at poor old Ichabod Crane. At the end of the tale, it's revealed the Headless Horseman's missile was most likely a pumpkin. When the scene plays out in the mind's eye, it's easy to imagine the Horseman's head as a glowing pumpkin with human features, something very close to Jack's old lantern. From there, it's a quick jump to carved and lit up pumpkins being named jack-o'-lanterns.

No matter its origins, the jack-o'-lantern serves as the nearly official symbol of the Samhain season. Glowing pumpkins gaze outward from porches in late October, scanning for trick-or-treaters, and pumpkin decorations haunt street corners and grocery stores. And for Witches, jack-o'-lanterns serve as a guidepost for the returning souls of our beloved dead, inviting those we've lost to be with us once more. Whether we carve them, eat them, decorate them, or use them in ritual, the pumpkin is one of autumn's most delightful gifts.

References

Morton, Ella. "Turnip Jack-o'-Lanterns Are the Root of All Evil." Atlas Obscura. October 28, 2015. https://www.atlasobscura.com/articles/turnip-jack-o-lanterns-are-the-root-of-all-evil.

Skal, David, J. *Death Makes a Holiday: A Cultural History of Halloween*. New York: Bloomsbury Books, 2002.

Feasts and Treats

Elizabeth Barrette

SAMHAIN IS THE DYING time, a holiday of death at the end of the growing season. Autumn is at its height, the trees red and gold in their slowly falling leaves. The orchards, having given up their fruit, prepare for the long winter sleep.

Pork Roast

Traditionally, pigs were slaughtered at Samhain, making pork a traditional feast food. Many cooking apples ripen in October, and root vegetables are available then. These represent many aspects of death, rebirth, and earth.

Prep time: 20 minutes
Cooking time: 4–6 hours
Servings: 5–7

2 cups apple cider
½ cup apple butter
2 tablespoons apple cider vinegar
1 bay leaf
½ teaspoon pink salt
½ teaspoon red peppercorns
¼ teaspoon ground cloves

¼ teaspoon paprika
1 tablespoon brown sugar
pork loin roast (4–5 pounds)
2 red apples, sliced
2 carrots, chopped
3 celery stalks, chopped
1 leek, sliced
1 teaspoon thyme
1 teaspoon sweet marjoram

Into a slow cooker, put 2 cups apple cider, ½ cup apple butter, 2 tablespoons apple cider vinegar, and 1 bay leaf. Cover and turn on low.

Grind together ½ teaspoon pink salt, ½ teaspoon red peppercorns, ¼ teaspoon ground cloves, and ¼ teaspoon paprika. Add 1 tablespoon brown sugar.

Rub the spice blend all over the pork roast. Put the pork roast in the crockpot and cover.

Rinse, core, and slice 2 red apples. Rinse 2 carrots and chop them into chunks. Rinse 3 celery stalks and chop them into chunks. Cut the root end off the leek. Slice the white part and as much of the light green as you can before it turns tough. Add all the cut produce to the crockpot, distributing it around the roast.

Over the top, sprinkle 1 teaspoon thyme and 1 teaspoon sweet marjoram. Cover and cook for 4–6 hours until vegetables are tender and pork starts to fall apart.

Autumn Orchard Crumble

Apples and pears are the quintessential fruits of autumn. They mingle beautifully in this Autumn Orchard Crumble. Warming spices such as cinnamon and ginger reflect the fire-colored leaves of autumn and counteract its cold weather.

Prep time: 45 minutes
Cooking time: 40–50 minutes
Serves: 8

butter

flour

2 firm cooking apples (like Granny Smith or Fuji)

1 soft cooking apple (like Jonathan or McIntosh)

2 teaspoons lemon juice

2 firm cooking pears (like Bosc or Anjou)

1 soft cooking pear (like Bartlett)

2 tablespoons ginger chips or minced candied ginger

1 teaspoon ground ginger

2 tablespoons white sugar

1 tablespoon tapioca starch

1 cup all-purpose flour

½ teaspoon cinnamon

¼ teaspoon ground cloves

¼ teaspoon allspice

¼ teaspoon sea salt

1 cup quick oats

1 cup sliced almonds

2 tablespoons flaxseed meal

½ cup brown sugar, firmly packed

½ cup unsalted butter, sliced (1 stick)

(For a gluten-free version, replace the all-purpose wheat flour with a gluten-free flour. For a nut-free version, replace the sliced almonds with sunflower seeds or pepitas.)

Preheat the oven to 350°F. Butter a pie plate or large baking dish. Sprinkle about a tablespoon of flour into the pie plate. Tilt and tap the pie plate to move the flour around until it coats the whole inside.

Wash and pat dry the apples. Remove the stems and cores. (If you like your pie apples peeled, do that now, but it's okay to leave the skin on.) Slice the apples thinly, but not so thin that the slices break easily. Put them in a large bowl. Sprinkle 1 teaspoon lemon juice over them and toss gently to coat the slices.

Wash and pat dry the pears. Remove the stems and cores. (If you like your pie pears peeled, do that now, but it's okay to leave the skin on.) Slice the pears thinly, but not so thin that the slices break easily. Add them to the bowl of apple slices. Sprinkle 1 teaspoon lemon juice over them and toss gently to coat the slices.

Add 2 tablespoons ginger chips or minced candied ginger, 1 teaspoon ground ginger, 2 tablespoons white sugar, and 1 tablespoon tapioca starch. Toss gently to coat the slices. Pour the fruit slices into the prepared pie plate and spread them out. Mound them slightly in the center and make sure that the outer edges stay below the rim of the pie plate, leaving room to add the crumble topping later.

In a large mixing bowl, sift together 1 cup all-purpose flour, ½ teaspoon cinnamon, ¼ teaspoon ground cloves, ¼ teaspoon allspice, and ¼ teaspoon sea salt.

To the flour mixture, add 1 cup quick oats, 1 cup sliced almonds, and 2 tablespoons flaxseed meal. Stir to combine.

To the flour mixture, add ½ cup of firmly packed brown sugar. Slice 1 stick of unsalted butter (½ cup) into the bowl. Use a butter cutter to combine the ingredients in the bowl. It helps to have a table knife to run between the tines of the butter cutter and knock loose the packed butter. Keep going until the mixture is loose, dry, and crumbly. The butter should be down to pea-sized bits.

Use a soup spoon to put the topping over the fruit, starting in the center and spiraling outward. Keep an eye on the amount so you don't run out of topping before covering the whole surface. When you get to the outside edge, put the spoon on the rim of the pie plate and tilt it inward to avoid spilling. If there is topping left over after covering the surface, look for any empty or thin spots in the topping and deposit the extra there. Otherwise, just distribute it evenly over the top.

Bake the Autumn Orchard Crumble at 350°F for 40–50 minutes until done. The crumble topping should be toasty brown and crisp, not wet. The fruit should be bubbling around the edges of the pie plate, and it should feel soft when a toothpick is inserted into the middle of the mound. If the topping seems to be browning faster than the fruit is softening, you can make a tent of aluminum foil to minimize further browning. Remove from the oven and allow to cool for at least 5 minutes before serving.

This recipe makes about 8 servings. Because a crumble dessert has no bottom crust, you will need to serve it with a spoon, not a pie server. Popular additions include vanilla or ginger ice cream or frozen yogurt, caramel sauce, ginger syrup, cinnamon syrup, or gingersnaps.

Pomegranate Punch

Pomegranate is the fruit of death, as apple is the fruit of life, celebrating both in this liminal time. Warming spices of ginger and cinnamon contrast with the cold beverage.

Prep time: 10 minutes
Cooking time: freeze ice cubes 4 hours
Servings: 13

pomegranate seeds
water
4 cups cold pomegranate juice
4 cups cold ginger beer (strong)
3 cups cold apple cider
1 cup cold cranberry juice
1 tablespoon pure cinnamon extract

Fill an ice cube tray with pomegranate seeds. Pour water over the seeds. Freeze until solid, about 4 hours.

In a large punch bowl, mix 4 cups cold pomegranate juice, 4 cups cold ginger beer, 3 cups cold apple cider, 1 cup cold cranberry juice, and 1 tablespoon pure cinnamon extract. Use the strongest ginger beer you can find, so it still has flavor when diluted. Serve over pomegranate ice cubes.

Crafty Crafts

Charlie Rainbow Wolf

SAMHAIN IS THE TIME of year when the veil between our reality and other realms is believed to be most transparent. It's the season when wearing masks and fancy dress to try to fool malevolent spirits into not recognizing us is popular, and when carved pumpkins or turnips for talismans of protection are seen on many doorsteps. It is also an occasion when many traditions reach out to connect with their ancestors.

So, what does a doll have to do with Samhain?

Spirit Dolls

A spirit doll is a sacred connection to a spiritual entity. It might embody the energy of a tree or a river, it could be made as an offering to a deceased loved one, or it may even be an homage to a spirit guide or patron god or goddess. They're particularly appropriate for Samhain, simply because the veil is the thinnest.

Spirit dolls are not a modern practice; they date back for centuries and are practiced by many cultures, but recently they're seeing a resurgence in popularity. Perhaps people are hungry to connect with something meaningful that returns them to their roots. It does not matter what path you walk or how you make the doll. The most important thing is your intent. Remember, you are calling an entity to come and dwell in the doll; create a comfortable and meaningful habitat.

Materials

It's hard to instruct you on exactly what to get, because every doll is different. The materials do not need to be expensive, and most can be found either in popular craft retailers or online shops. The list below is a sample of what might be used; the actual components are left to your creativity, and not everything listed will be needed.

Something for the face: An old doll head or perhaps a form made from a mold.

Fabric or wadding for the body: Straw, polyester, or scraps of material all work.

Fabric or other materials to dress the doll: Let your imagination run with this one!

Something for the stability: Any kind of stick—and this might even be optional.

Inclusions: What you want to put in the doll—herbs, crystals, amulets.

A needle and thread: Sharp needles and quilter's thread recommended.

Glue: I like Elmer's or tacky.

Embellishments: Think about charms or other items that help identify the doll's purpose.

Cost: From absolutely nothing to over $50; it's subject to what you have and what you want to spend.

Time spent: Anywhere from an hour to several days, depending on how deeply you want to involve yourself.

Birth Your Doll

As you start to gather the materials, think carefully about the spirit you want to embody in the doll. Is it a nature spirit? A guide or guardian? An ancestor? Just as different people have different personalities, your spirit doll needs to reflect the personality of the

spirit you are inviting. Of course, allow any glue or additional paint to dry.

You might want your spirit doll to be made up of natural components—although if you already have polyester stuffing and nylon fabric, you're not breaking any rules. Intent is everything. Many items can be wild-harvested, especially if you live in a rural area. Ensure you have permission either from the landowner or from the nature spirits to take what calls to you.

The doll requires a sturdy form for the materials to be wrapped around. Sticks work, as do dowel rods if sticks are not available. I'm an avid knitter, and I have a plethora of odd or wonky knitting needles and crochet hooks—yard sale finds, or given to me by others when they were getting rid of their craft items, etc. These are the "bones" of my spirit doll.

The doll also needs a body, something to give it form and shape. I have seen straw and florists moss used, but I wonder about the durability of these, especially if the spirit doll is to last longer than a season or two. I'm keen on recycling, so I tend to scavenge old t-shirts from my friends and family, cutting them into long strips and then wrapping them around the stick form until I get the desired shape. It's possible to give the spirit doll arms by attaching a smaller stick perpendicular to the larger one, but I don't bother with this. By the time I have clothed my spirit doll, the additional limbs are not missed.

Inclusions such as herbs or crystals or charms should be added now, wrapping them in the body materials and making sure they are secure. Anything that helps you to tell the story of the doll or enhance its purpose is appropriate. I can't say it enough: it all comes down to intent. I frequently add sage or cedar to the spirit dolls I make. According to Scott Cunningham, sage represents protection, longevity, and wisdom (Cunningham 1985, n.p.). Cedar also offers protection and purification (Cunningham 1985, n.p.). My Cherokee friends say cedar represents the ancestors.

Once the doll has form, it's time to add the face. This is probably the most important part of the doll, for this is where it gets its character. Being a potter, I make clay faces for my dolls and attach them to the wrapped t-shirt body with a bit of glue—or, more recently, I've been making holes in the clay before firing it, so I can sew the faces onto the body. It's possible to use old fashioned doll faces, or make an original face out of clay; air-dried clay works just fine. Free form the face or use a mold—usually available in the same section of the craft store as the polymer clay. The face could even be stitched or painted directly onto the body fabric; there's no right or wrong way to do this.

Finally, the doll needs dressing. This is the fun part! Add bits of lace, crochet, knitting, fabric, moss, leaves, twigs, beads; the choices are infinite. Let the doll reflect both you as its creator and the spirit you are honoring. The face gives the doll expression, but the clothing is where the doll comes to life with personality and purpose. If the fabric seems to need more shape or form, it can be starched or immersed in watered-down glue or even have florist's wire threaded through it. Add any accoutrements for the doll to wear at this time, such as jewelry, charms, or other items.

Does the doll want wings or multiple limbs or more than one head? Let your imagination run riot and see where it takes you. You're connecting with the other realms; ask the spirits what they seek of you, then let your hands reflect the message. It's been my experience that making the dolls doesn't just connect me to another entity; each one also allows me to explore a different aspect of myself.

Your spirit doll has the potential to become your friend, confidant, and ally. After all, it is an expression of your true nature; it is something you have created with your heart and your soul as well as your hands. It was born from an idea in your mind and came into being through your own actions. Treat it with respect and see it as an extension of both yourself and your faith.

Further Reading

The Healing Doll Way: A Guided Process Creating Art Dolls for Self-Discovery, Awareness, and Transformation by Barb Kobe, 2018.

How to Create a Spirit Doll by Chris Flynn, 2014.

Soul Mate Dolls: Dollmaking as a Healing Art by Noreen Crone-Findlay, 2000.

Reference

Cunningham, Scott. *Cunningham's Encyclopedia of Magical Herbs.* St. Paul, MN: Llewellyn Publications, 1985.

Candle Magic

Ember Grant

SAMHAIN, WHICH CONTAINS THE roots of our modern Halloween, is one of the most significant celebrations of the year. The word means "summer's end" but it's much more than that. It is believed that the way to the otherworld is easier to access during this time. This is also the final harvest of the season and a time to set aside stores of food for the winter.

Memorial Candle

While the ancient Celts certainly considered this an important time of year, we can't be certain if they honored ancestors on this night. Regardless, it has become a custom for many modern Wiccans, Witches, and Pagans to perform rituals at Samhain for ancestors. For this ritual, you will create a candle to honor a departed loved one using a sigil created specifically for that person.

The act of creating a sigil is part of the magic. Burning it, in this case on a candle, releases its energy. There are many ways to create a sigil, and the preparation is a key part of the ritual.

In this case, you're creating a symbol that expresses something about the person you wish to honor. Of course, you could just write that person's name on a candle, but where's the symbolism in that?

Go deeper and incorporate things that remind you of that person's character.

One easy way is to combine the person's initials with simple symbols of things they loved. For example, I have an aunt whose initials are S. G. W. F. T. (first name, middle initial, maiden name, and two married names). You can use more or fewer letters. Practice on paper first. Find a way to link the letters together. Next, think of things he or she enjoyed. My aunt loved owls. I could draw an outline of an owl into the sigil or just a pair of large owl eyes. She was a singer and loved music, so I could add a music note too. You get the idea. Spend some time creating the sigil and, when you have it perfected, you can begin the spell and carve it into the candle.

You can use a taper or votive candle, but it may be easier to carve on a larger one, such as a pillar size. The choice is yours. White is a good color for this candle, but you can also use brown or black.

You can make several of these—one for each person you wish to honor—and decorate your altar with other mementos such as photos, special items, and flowers. You can honor relatives, friends—anyone you wish, even if it's not someone you knew personally but admired from afar. As long as you have a way to convey that person's name and something of their personality to the candle, it works. The goal is to celebrate the life of someone you miss.

Anoint the candle and engrave it with a crystal point or other tool of your choice. The point is to focus your energy while creating the sigil and then allow the candle to burn out.

As you light each one, say these words and insert the name of the person you're honoring.

Light the way for (person's name), wherever (he/she/they) may be; their memory lives on, they are part of me.

Follow this by saying whatever other words you desire. Let the candles burn out or relight them each night until they do.

Candle Divination

We often associate Samhain with divination, and that's because it has deep roots in history. Samhain "was more celebrated for divination than any other night of the year" for the Celtic people (Hutton 1997, loc 8648).

If you haven't tried the technique of wax divination, experiment with it this year. You'll need a bowl of cold water and a taper candle. The idea is to drip wax into the bowl and interpret the shape of the wax droplets. This type of divination is called carromancy or ceromancy and it has been practiced for thousands of years. Many practitioners also study the way the candle burns as part of the divination process, studying the flame itself, as well as the shape of the candle and wax pool. Wax that hardens on the side of the candle and in the container can be interpreted as well.

Think of a specific question before you begin. If you wish, choose a candle color that corresponds with your question—green for wealth, pink for love and relationships, orange for success, yellow for communication, blue for health and healing, and red for protection. Of course, you can always use white as an all-purpose color.

Burning is the easy part. What most people find challenging is interpreting the results. As with all forms of divination, people will "see" different things. This is personal, and you should keep in mind that the future is never defined for us. Divination gives us hints and whispers about possibility. It's a way to explore.

Here are some standard interpretations:

• To interpret hardened wax, don't overanalyze. What comes to your mind first upon seeing the image? How does that relate to your question?

• A flame that is steady and unwavering, tall, and strong is a signal of success. Clean-burning, without residue is also a good sign.

- If the flame is weak or very small, you may need to try again. You may need to project more energy. But wait and see—sometimes a weak flame is just a slow start. Or you can start over with a different candle.
- Sounds that occur, including hissing and popping or crackling, can be signs of a message trying to reach you. Look for other signs and signals.
- Smoke can be different signs as well. Generally, white or gray smoke is positive but black is negative.
- If the flame flickers erratically and there's no obvious cause such as wind, you may need to focus harder on your intent. It could also be a sign of indecision. You can also study the flame's movement for shapes or other signs.
- If the flame goes out immediately for no apparent reason, this is a signal that the time is not right and you should try again later.
- Uneven burning that is not attributed to air flow could be a sign of opposition. Try again later.

These are not the only interpretations. Study a variety of sources and, most importantly, use your own intuition. Of course, remember that the type of candle you're using, how it's made, the type of wick, the size, shape, and type of container, the atmosphere and environment, all play a role in how a candle burns. Nothing is certain, especially in divination. But it's a fun way to explore the possibilities; keep an open mind.

Reference
Hutton, Ronald. *Stations of the Sun: A History of the Ritual Year in Britain.* Oxford University Press: New York. Kindle edition, 1997.

Samhain Ritual

Natalie Zaman

IN GIORGIO VASARI'S *The Lives of the Most Excellent Painters, Sculptors, and Architects,* the biographer describes a moment in the life of Leonardo da Vinci in which young Leonardo's father asked him to "paint something" on a round piece of wood. True to character, da Vinci brought this "canvas" to his room to work in secret—along with the carcasses of "lizards great and small, crickets, serpents, butterflies, grasshoppers, bats, and other strange kinds of suchlike animals" (Vasari, 287). These he cobbled together into a Franken-creature that, according to Vasari was, "most horrible and terrifying, which emitted a poisonous breath and turned the air to flame" (Vasari, 287). The shape of the wood was shield-like; what better protection for a knight in battle than his very own personal monster?

Whatever inspired da Vinci to create an image so terrible, I would guess that there was some humor in it, albeit the dark kind, the same that can be found in the Samhainishly creepy animal-masked citizens of Summerisle in the original *Wicker Man* film (though they are celebrating Beltane), or the fantastic world populated with human-beasts in Laini Taylor's *Daughter of Smoke and Bone* where it was more desirable to have a human face, whatever combination of animal limbs were concocted to house the soul. The spirit of drolleries lives on.

Drolleries appeared in the margins of books—an unexpected surprise, disturbing perhaps, and set there to provoke thought. But what if these curious creatures could step out of their pages and invite you to join their dance?

The Monster's Ball

The following ritual can be done as a group activity or by a solitary practitioner and unfolds as a five-act play, for you shall don a disguise, act, disrobe, and emerge changed. Use the structure as a guide; as a ritual and craft it can be as simple or as elaborate as you wish to make it. The one thing that is nonnegotiable is the use of recyclable materials, for reasons that you will soon see.

Items needed:

Magenta candle (Magenta is a color often associated with transformation, the heart of this work. Magenta imbibes passionate red and thoughtful purple, which will help focus your energy.)

Myrrh essential oil (Myrrh promotes relaxation, which will aid in the meditation act of the ritual. In the ancient world, myrrh was a luxury item, much like the illuminated books in which drolleries are found. Used in embalming, it is a nod to Samhain, the season of shadow celebrated at this time.)

Scissors

Recyclable materials such as magazines, newspapers, cardboard, and paper bags

Stapler

Masking tape

Glue stick

Journal

Pencils or other writing implements

Mirror

Optional: Music to play in the background and set the mood. Because this work is inspired by British and European medieval art, I prefer British or European medieval music such as The Cambridge Singers' *Brother Sun, Sister Moon*, or any music by Anonymous 4.

Before you begin, cleanse and create your sacred space, making sure to have all of your materials set up so that they are accessible. While the descriptions of each "act" of this ritual are brief, take the time you need to experience each fully. You will know when the time is right to move on to the next phase. Feel free to change up any details in this ritual to suit your needs.

The Meditation

Dress the magenta candle with the myrrh and light it. Breathing deeply, stare into the flame and visualize a pair of eyes forming around it:

> *Cat eyes,*
> *Snake eyes,*
> *Doe eyes,*
> *Come!*
> *From the darkness what shall emerge?*

Visualize a face and body forming around the eyes and emerging from the darkness—this is your creature, the skin you will create and put on. Don't try to think about it too much, just be aware of the first shape or shapes that come to mind. Perhaps what you see is a combination of animals or creatures; it may be that what you see has no name or is unidentifiable. Write down a description or draw it if it will help you remember.

The Creation

Using the recyclable materials, craft a guise for yourself in the shape of the creature that came to you in the meditation. It might be a single creature or a combination of several: animal, human, and plant.

Take a moment to sketch out some ideas if you have not done so already. Don't worry about being artistic or perfect; your purpose is to channel the energy you received in the mediation to create the being that you will become. Once you have a solid picture of what your guise will be, begin putting it together. You can craft a mask or a headband, a tail, coverings for your limbs, scales, or fur. Make your guise as simple or as elaborate as you like.

The Transformation

Carefully put on your guise. (Have extra tape or other means of repair close by in case of rips and tears.) Once you're completely kitted out, take the time you need to get used to yourself in your new skin. Look in the mirror. What do you see? How does it feel to be this new creature? Be aware of your feelings: Are you scared? Bold? Confused? If you are able, write your feelings down. Next, find your voice. Speak in your new tongue. You may not understand it at first but keep talking. If you're in a group, speak to each other. Keep in mind that animals use other speech besides sound: they posture, dance, and touch. When you are comfortable in your new skin, parade around your sacred space. Dance! This is the Monster's Ball! Walk and speak and gesture as you are now. What do you have to say?

The Unmasking

Taking off your guise is just as important as putting it on. Disrobing, stripping away what covers you, can be humbling, exhilarating, freeing, and frightening all at the same time. Take a moment to find yourself underneath your new skin, then, slowly, take it off, one piece at a time. Follow your instincts—what comes off first? As you take off each piece, give thanks and lay it down reverently; perhaps you will arrange it into the shape as you remember yourself in it. Just as you did when you put on this guise, be aware of your feelings and write them down if it helps you articulate and remember them.

The Release

This is, for me, the most powerful part of the ritual. It is not easy to let go of something you've created, or even something (or someone) you have become. One of the lessons that Samhain teaches us is the temporary nature of life. Think of everything you can that is attached to the guise you have created and put on. Why do you think this is what you needed to become for this single night or hour? What lesson did it present to you; what is it asking you to consider in the coming year? Collect your creation and look at it with these words before you put it into the flames:

No longer am I what I was,
And I release the past because
The past is past,
The future unknown
The present, I know, is my true home.

Keep the fire going until the entire guise is reduced to ash. Let the ashes cool and settle overnight, then scatter them in the light of the morning. As the year continues to wane and then wax into spring, remember drolleries and the Monster's Ball and draw on their energy when you encounter shadows in corners and rustles in the undergrowth of the New Year.

Further Reading and Viewing

Hardy, Robin, dir. *The Wicker Man*. Edward Woodward, Christopher Lee, Diane Cilento. British Lion Film Corporation, 1973.

Taylor, Laini. *Daughter of Smoke and Bone*. New York: Little Brown and Company, 2011.

Reference

Vasari, Giorgio. *The Lives of the Most Excellent Painters, Sculptors, and Architects*. Translated by Gaston du C. de Vere. Edited by Philip Jacks. New York: Modern Library, 2006.

Notes

Notes

Notes

Yule

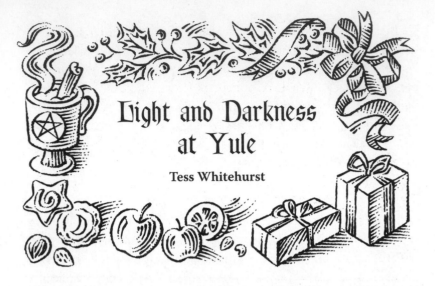

Light and Darkness at Yule

Tess Whitehurst

MIDWINTER: IS IT ONE of the most magical nights of the year, or is it *the* most magical night of the year? While the answer to this question will vary depending on which Witch you ask, there's no denying that Yule has a deep and profound magic all its own. As the Wheel of the Year reaches its coldest, darkest point, we feel spiritually drawn to merge with our inner Midwinter: to anchor ourselves in silence, and to connect with the womb of creation, in which all is conceived, from which all is born.

And from this point of deepest darkness, the light of the world—the sun—is born anew. Just as deep sleep engenders vital energy and a quiet mind gives birth to brilliant ideas and transcendent works of art, the profound darkness of icy Midwinter coincides with the astrological rebirth of the star at the center of our solar system that bathes our world in brightness and causes all our food and flowers to grow. Once Midwinter arrives, we know that each day will bring more and more sunlight. As the wheel turns upward toward the other polarity of the year, we know our hearts and spirits, which have been buried like seeds under the snow of the season, will slowly begin to stir and unfurl as they are bathed in the incrementally increasing radiance of each passing day.

Because our bodies and spirits sense this, Midwinter sparks joy within us. The other reason Midwinter sparks joy is because the relentless cold and darkness compel us to spark our own joy and find our own warmth. We do this through ritual, tradition, song, scent, light, food, family, and friendship. And by stoking our own inner light and surrounding ourselves with coziness and beauty, we remind ourselves that we possess the fortifying, celebratory power of the sun within our very hearts.

An Ancient and Modern Deity

I grew up in the Central Valley of California, where it virtually never snows. When I was a child of six, my mom packed my three-year-old brother and me in her Ford Escort and took us to her childhood home in the Sierra Nevada Mountains for our first white Christmas. Sometime in the middle of the night, as my brother and I slept in a creaky bed that smelled like antique books, I heard a distant bell. I climbed up to my knees to peek out the second story window and was delighted, if not entirely surprised, to see Santa, his sled, and all his reindeer parked in the snow. The details are a little fuzzy, but I want to say he was checking his bag of gifts or feeding his reindeer or engaging in some other such routine maintenance. I shook my little brother, and when he woke up, I whispered, "Look!" He stood up on the bed so he could see out too. We watched silently in awe for just a few moments, with the feeling that we were seeing something we weren't supposed to. Then we gingerly returned to our pillows, doing our best not to be noticed by the magical beings outside.

To this day, we both still remember this event. Over the years, we have periodically checked in with each other: "Remember when we saw Santa?" And the answer is always yes. That happened and we agree: Santa is real and so are his reindeer. Many have suggested or implied that we were dreaming or that our shared memory is otherwise not reliable. But this has never been the least bit convincing to us. Our minds are made up.

While this was of course December 24 and not technically Yuletide, every sabbat is a portal, and the Yule portal was open. And, like all young minds, ours were awake to magic. As opposed to adult magical practitioners who intentionally cultivate the magical consciousness through things like meditation and ritual, magic was the only consciousness we knew. We had not yet been indoctrinated to the illusion of separation, so for us there was no veil to be lifted between seen and unseen, known and unknown, "real" and "imagined." There were no two worlds to walk between: there was only one unified consciousness, where we existed and Santa and his reindeer did too.

Santa is a modern name for a divinity with much more ancient roots. His red and white clothing and association with reindeer have caused some scholars to convincingly argue that he is inspired by historic Arctic shamans who used *Amanita muscaria* (the classic red and white polka-dotted psychedelic mushroom) to access magical consciousness. He is also associated with Catholicism's St. Nicholas, who was famous for his generosity, as well as the Norse god Odin, who led the Wild Hunt, the legendary parade of spirits that soars through the Midwinter sky at night.

While some magical practitioners consider Santa to be something of a cartoon character and even a commercial invention (a 1930s ad by the Coca-Cola Company is often cited as the origin of his present-day costume), to me, his modern incarnation is only further proof of his existence. A magical spirit honored in the aggressively secular and utilitarian realm we call the modern world? That's as stubbornly enduring as they come. Children basically worship him, and even the least magically minded adults among us invoke his name and likeness for purposes ranging from attracting more money (e.g., "mall Santas") to inspiring generosity (e.g., white beard bedecked Goodwill bell ringers) to making our children behave (e.g., his naughty and nice list).

When you consider Yuletide's attributes—coldness, darkness, and the rebirth of the light—it's easy to see why Santa has been such an enduring fixture. He is warm, jolly, and generous: qualities that remind us of the brightness within us as well as the return of the sun. What's more, Santa's famous laugh and munificent nature are reminiscent of the Roman god Jupiter, whose corresponding planet is the ruler of sparkly, bighearted Sagittarius, where the sun dwells during Yuletide season. But the darkness of Yuletide is a part of Santa's nature as well: he lives at the planet's coldest, darkest point (the North Pole), and his identification with Odin (not to mention the hallucinogenic experiences of arctic shamans) reveals more hidden associations with death, transformation, alchemy, rebirth, inner journeying, and deep magical lore.

The Contrast and Paradox of Yule

Like Santa, Yule is simultaneously bright and dark, expansive and introspective, active and still. At first glance, the celebratory aspects of the season are obvious, while its more mysterious and alchemical aspects are hidden beneath its glittery surface. With the sun at its lowest ebb, the Yule season inspires us to find the light within our hearts, which in turn can cast an even darker shadow. For example, decorations and songs are at their campiest at this time of year (think ugly sweater parties, elaborate holiday light displays, and cloyingly cheery holiday carols). But having grown up in a funeral chapel family, I happen to know what the holiday season is called in that industry: "busy season." True story. It's not only the Wheel of the Year's symbolic death and rebirth, it's also the time when people literally die the most often, whether it's from illness, loneliness, or cold.

It speaks to the unstoppable power of this stark polarity that even mainstream holiday myths illuminate this theme, and always with magical overtones. Consider just three of our most beloved holiday stories: *A Christmas Carol*, *It's a Wonderful Life*, and *The Nightmare Before Christmas*. In the first, the main character is near the end of his life and is visited by spirits and ghosts. In the second, the main character is about to kill himself. And in the third, the aesthetics of Halloween (Samhain) and Christmas (Yule) are juxta-posed, illuminating the oft-overlooked darkness of the latter. It's no coincidence that these are the stories that resonate so deeply with so many at this time of year.

As Pagans, we know that Yule is not only literally darker than Samhain (i.e., the days are shorter and nights are longer), but it's also spiritually darker. While Samhain translates to "summer's end" and is the transition from the light half of the Celtic year to the dark half, Yule is the deepest and darkest moment within the heart of the dark half. It's not just that the light is dying, it's that the light is (symbolically) dead. Solstice translates to "sun stands still," and indeed, just for a moment, we feel its lowest ebb as a figurative death. Perhaps that's why the playfulness of Samhain does not accompany the dark aspects of Yule. Yes, we celebrate the return of the light. But we don't feel as warm and fuzzy about the otherworld souls of the Wild Hunt riding through the night sky as we do about, for example, sugar skulls at Día de los Muertos and dumb suppers at Samhain. To summarize, Yule is less of a the-veil-is-thin feeling and more of a the-veil-is-a-gaping-hole feeling. No wonder we want to gather around the Yule log and sing cheerful songs.

At the same time, it's that very darkness that makes the light shine so brightly. Scrooge's Christmas morning wouldn't have been so dazzling if it hadn't been for his archetypal dark night of the soul. If George Bailey hadn't been about to jump from that bridge, his reunion with his family and townsfolk could never have been so joyous. And of course, this Yuletide chiaroscuro is also present in the most literal sense: candles, hearth fires, and holiday lights are naturally more luminous in the darkest and coldest of nights.

Honoring the Dark While Welcoming the Light

One of the most beautiful aspects of the magical spiritual path is our willingness to gaze into the darkness, even as we celebrate the light. We know that we can't leave death out of the cycle of life, not just because we are powerless to do so, but also because death paves the way for gestation, transformation, and rebirth. Similarly, when we deny our darker thoughts and less positive emotions, we cut ourselves off from the full range of human experience. We may dull our sadness, but we simultaneously diminish our joy. You can't numb one without numbing the other. It is only by fully allowing all of it, breathing through it, and making peace with the contrast that we find true balance, harmony, power, and flow.

At Midsummer, Yule's polarity, we celebrate the fullness of the sun's power. On the other hand, at Yule, we often talk about celebrating the rebirth of the light. And celebrating the rebirth of the light is great, but it's important to also celebrate Midsummer's polarity: the full flowering of the dark. While we may be tempted to fill every waking hour during Yule season with some sort of activity or task, this is the time when we feel most naturally like resting, listening to silence, contemplating the mystery, and going within. Just as Midsummer comes with the impulse to dance, laugh, and toast to the sun, if you look deeply, you will find that Midwinter comes with the instinct to become very still in order to salute the dark and fertile womb of creation, the absolute void, the place to which we are all one day destined to return (on the day of our death), and from which—like the sun—we are all destined to be once again reborn.

The true spirit of Yule guides us to make friends with stillness, silence, rest, death, and the dark womb of creation. If we do so bravely and reverently, this will not mire us in depression or fear but will ultimately guide us toward being symbolically reborn. Much like the Sumerian goddess Inanna, who willingly plunged into the underworld, we will be empowered to cleanse and consecrate our spirits, fortify ourselves with wisdom and power, and reemerge gloriously into the light.

Cosmic Sway

Robin Ivy Payton

THE WHEEL OF THE Year begins with Yule and festivals of light. Familiar among these holidays are Hanukkah, Christmas, Yuletide, and Solstice during the months from November to January. Merriment, gift giving, and traditional foods are unifying elements of these various celebrations.

The Sun shifts to Capricorn on December 21, the Winter Solstice, at 10:59 a.m. EST. Astrological winter begins, and we honor the goddess for rejuvenating light. On this shortest day, some also acknowledge Father Time. The earth has been dormant for many weeks, and the newly re-birthed Sun prepares to warm and awaken the ground. After long nights of darkness since Samhain, now daylight will slowly increase. There's both promise and patience in this holiday as light consumes darkness incrementally. Fireplaces are lit and bonfires blaze, reminding us that warmth and sunshine will naturally return. Midwinter, as it's known, has arrived.

Astrology of Midwinter

Winter Solstice occurs on December 21, about two days after Gemini Full Moon. The Moon is void of course in Cancer from 9:44 a.m. until 4:53 p.m. EST. Only simple, straightforward business and tasks are favored during these hours when things may be forgotten, misjudged, or taken for granted. Time important discussions or agreements for before or after this transition. Leo Moon moves in for festive feelings, social gatherings, and celebrations of light this evening. Include children in your traditions, as they are ruled by Leo Moon. Creative tasks such as wreath making, tree decorating, and baking emphasize the earth element of Capricorn, now graced by Mercury, Venus, and the Sun.

Christmas Eve and Day

The Moon moves to Virgo for December 24 and lingers there through Christmas Day. A majority of heavenly bodies, including Sun and Moon, travel the earth signs for this year's Christmas. One advantage and benefit is emotional grounding. Guests will appreciate what's familiar and comfortable, though in the case of quick changes, Virgo Moon means versatility. It's a friendly looking day, as Mercury aligns with the Moon. From gift giving to dinner planning, the vibe is down to earth.

New and Full Moons

Sagittarius New Moon is also a total solar eclipse on December 4, visible in the Southern Hemisphere. Eclipses accelerate change and often bring unexpected realizations, developments, and announcements. With solar eclipses, expect beginnings and arrivals. More powerful than a usual New Moon, the eclipse will prompt learning, travels, and shifting ways of life. Sagittarius is a sign of expanding knowledge and experience. The solar eclipse helps free the mind for either or both, while planet Mercury highlights exciting ideas.

This solar eclipse happens during Hanukkah, the festival of lights timed near the New Moon closest to Solstice. This year's eight nights of Hanukkah are November 28 to December 6. Eight candles on a menorah are lit, one by one, and a blessing recited each night. As this Jewish holiday has its own unique meaning, it also shares the spirit and symbolism of light with other winter feasts.

The New to Full Moon cycle may seem to pass quickly and eventfully. Sagittarius and Gemini, the mutable signs involved, indicate movement and change. The solar eclipse adds to that effect, with one development after another leading to the Full Moon on December 18. Jupiter is an influencer, highlighting community and humanitarian efforts. Forward thinking, innovative qualities shine through during Full Moon. And with Jupiter in altruistic and social Aquarius, parties and fundraisers are well timed for this Saturday night.

New Year's Eve and Day

As we bid adieu to 2021 and begin 2022, the Moon is waning in Sagittarius. This is favorable for reflecting, reimagining, and powerful intention setting as the New Moon in Capricorn approaches. Since the Moon and Mars are close together on New Year's Eve, avoid debates or conflicts that could become heated. Instead, bask in Sagittarius warmth, enthusiasm, and sense of adventure. Cultural experiences such as museum tours, art openings, and celebrations of diversity are well timed during Sagittarius Moon.

On January's first full day, a relaxed approach and unstructured time is best while the Moon is void of course from 3:16 a.m. to 6:01 p.m. EST. Capricorn Moon follows, leading to New Moon on January 2 at 1:33 p.m. On the twelfth degree of Capricorn, this meeting of Sun and Moon suggests learning and sharing of natural wisdom, referred to in the Sabian symbols as the "little known aspects of life" ("Look Up a Symbol"). In your resolutions or in problem solving, consider what the earth provides and what is readily available. Plants are resources for food and supplements, and animals make excellent teachers. Structured plans and practical goals are favored by this Capricorn Moon.

Astrology and the Tarot

Create a Yule or New Year's spell with tarot cards from the major arcana. Choose cards with light images for hope and renewal. The

Hermit resembles Father Time, linked to Capricorn and Saturn. The traditional card shows an old man with a bright lantern, a beacon in the otherwise gray atmosphere. When seeking solutions or the right path, use the Hermit to recall answers that come from within. Add the Star, a beautiful card for reemerging and inviting possibilities. Meditate upon the Star as you design and envision your future. And consider the World card for closure on the calendar year and the Fool for starting anew. Set these or other cards on an altar or sill to bathe in celestial light.

Reference

"Look Up a Symbol." Sabian Symbols by Lynda Hill. Accessed August 21, 2020. https://sabiansymbols.com/symbol-lookup/.

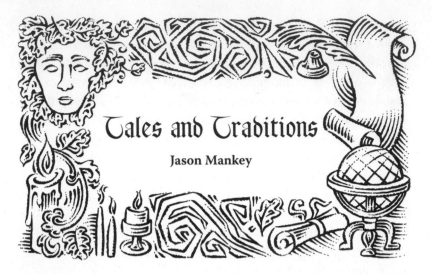

Tales and Traditions

Jason Mankey

WHILE IT'S TRUE THAT the ancient Norse celebrated a holiday called Yule, the ancient celebrations that have had the biggest impact on the modern celebration of the Winter Solstice come from the old Roman Empire. The customs and traditions associated with the holidays of both Saturnalia and the January Kalends have continued into the present day as a part of Pagan celebrations and as a part of Christian celebrations of Christmas. This holiday season, take the opportunity to make merry like a Roman, because you were probably going to do so anyways.

Yule: Make Merry Like a Roman

Saturnalia is far more famous than its January cousin, and for good reason. It's most likely been celebrated since 300 BCE and might be even older than that! Saturnalia was originally a one-day holiday celebrated on December 17 but was eventually extended into a week-long event lasting until December 23 (which, not surprisingly, includes the time of the Winter Solstice). Saturnalia was originally celebrated in honor of the Roman agricultural deity Saturn (Kronos in Greek mythology) and was primarily a time for feasting and merrymaking. Celebrations of Saturnalia continued officially in some places until the year 500 CE, and since Christmas looks an awful lot like Saturnalia, one can argue that they never really stopped.

The most important elements of a good Saturnalia celebration were eating and drinking, and doing both to the point of excess. Elaborate meals were served on all the days of the Saturnalia, and everyone, no matter their station in life, took part. At its heart, Saturnalia was a harvest festival, so most meals featured wheat bread in abundance. Ham remains a popular main course at many winter feasts, and the Romans might be the reason why. The Roman writer Martial commented in his work *Epigrams* that a pig "will make you a good Saturnalia" and pork sausages were a popular gift over the holiday (Manning 2002, 363). Saturnalia was also a time for tasty desserts, many made from apples and pears (which were in season) and sweetened with honey.

Drinking was a major part of Saturnalia, so much so that we even have a recipe for Saturnalia Wine dating back to the first century CE from the Roman writer Marcus Gavius Apicius. Saturnalia wine was sweet and was made by boiling wine and honey together and then adding dried fruit such as raisins, dates, or figs (so far so good right?) before adding spices that today are not generally added to wine. While the honey and wine were boiling, Romans would also add a generous amount of black pepper and often saffron and bay leaves. The result is something unexpected to the modern palate.

Drinking during the Saturnalia was such a part of the holiday that when Christmas took over after the Christianization of the Roman Empire, the booze continued to flow. Wine remained an important part of the new holiday, and as Christianity spread, other alcoholic drinks such as wassail (generally made from apple cider) and lambswool (made from frothy beer and apples) and eggnog became a part of holiday festivities. While most Witches don't engage in heavy drinking at Yule, the Romans' love of alcohol remains a part of the holiday season. New Year's Eve is especially booze-soaked, as are many office holiday parties. Things really haven't changed that much from two-thousand years ago!

One of the longest lasting holiday traditions that stems from the celebration of Saturnalia is the idea of "misrule." Misrule has many meanings but is basically synonymous with upsetting the established social order. During Roman celebrations of Saturnalia, slave owners would wait on their slaves, and those who were generally seen as being on the bottom rung of society often found themselves in positions of power (at least for a little while). Over the centuries this tradition would evolve into customs involving "Bean Kings" (and Queens) and Lords of Misrule, which generally involved average citizens lording over both their peers and the nobility.

The Roman Empire's richest citizens didn't engage in Saturnalia charity simply out of the goodness of their hearts, they participated because they were expected to! Changing the status quo between rich and poor, and master and slave, acted as a social safety valve, easing tensions between the haves and the have-nots. This part of Saturnalia would spread throughout Europe and can be found in English wassailing traditions and the American custom of trick or treating at Halloween.

Misrule expressed itself in other ways too. During the Saturnalia, both men and women were encouraged to cross-dress, upsetting long-established Roman social norms. "Dressing up" would continue to be a part of the holiday season long after the end of the Roman Empire as masquerades and other similar amusements became a part of many European noble courts. Holiday mock nobility was a long-lasting tradition in many parts of Europe, but eventually started to fade away at the start of the nineteenth century.

Saturnalia continues its hold over modern-day Yule celebrations in other ways too. Due to its proximity to (and often overlap with) the Winter Solstice, it became a time to welcome back the reborn sun. In addition, most of the decorations we use today during the holidays were popular at Saturnalia. Holly and ivy were common

Saturnalia decorations, and while the Romans did not take entire trees into their homes, they did decorate with pine branches and wreaths. The Romans also liked to sing bawdy carols at Saturnalia, a tradition that eventually evolved into "Christmas carols," which are often reimagined in Witch circles as songs dedicated to Yule.

Saturnalia was also a time to exchange gifts, but the January Kalends might have been an even more popular time for the custom. The Romans celebrated the start of every month (which they called kalends or calends), but the start of the New Year was especially festive. The Saturnalia decorations stayed on doors and mantles, and people indulged in yet another day dedicated to food and drink and, most interestingly, spent the days leading up to the January Kalends shopping.

The fourth-century Roman writer Libanius (314–c. 394) once commented that at the January Kalends, "The impulse to spend seizes everyone … People are not only generous towards themselves, but also towards their fellow-men. A stream of presents pours itself out on all sides" (Forbes 2007, 28). Just like many modern Witches, the Romans loved to exchange gifts as well at the start of winter!

If your Yule celebrations as a Witch this Yuletide are riotous and joyous, then you'll be taking a page directly from the Pagans of ancient Rome! So sing that song and drink that eggnog! The still-living traditions of Saturnalia and the January Kalends are the easiest way to connect with our Pagan past.

References

Forbes, Bruce David. *Christmas: A Candid History*. Berkeley, CA: University of California Press, 2007.

Mankey, Jason. *Llewellyn's Little Book of Yule*. Woodbury, MN: Llewellyn Publications, 2020.

Manning, John. *The Emblem*. London, UK: Reaktion Books, 2002.

Feasts and Treats

Elizabeth Barrette

YULE IS THE LONGEST night of the year. The cold and the dark are at their strongest. The light and heat of summer lie far away. So we gather and celebrate to create our own brightness.

Holiday Ham and Bean Soup

This is a quick recipe using hearty ingredients like ham, beans, and vegetables. Red and green bell peppers provide a festive topping and contrast with softer ingredients.

Prep time: 5 minutes
Cooking time: about 30 minutes
Servings: 10

4 cups vegetable broth
1 tablespoon garam masala
1 teaspoon whole black peppercorns
1 bay leaf
2 cups cooked ham, cubed
1 freezer package (16 ounces) mixed vegetables, thawed
2 cans (15 ounces) black-eyed peas
2 cans (15 ounces) navy beans

1 red bell pepper, diced
1 green bell pepper, diced

In a large soup pot, combine 4 cups vegetable broth, 1 table-spoon garam masala, 1 teaspoon whole black peppercorns, and 1 bay leaf. Turn on high.

Add 2 cups cubed cooked ham and 1 package thawed mixed vegetables. Open the 4 cans. Drain and rinse the black-eyed peas and the navy beans. Stir them into the soup.

Bring the soup to a boil. Reduce heat and simmer for 15 minutes.

Dice 1 red bell pepper and 1 green bell pepper. Mix the bits together. Top the soup with the peppers.

Winter Solstice Salad

Salads are thought of primarily as a summer food. However, some greens and other produce reach their peak in winter. This salad combines winter leaves with red and green leaves, plus a few toppings for interest.

Prep time: 45 minutes

Servings: 6 (2-cup) main salads or 12 (1-cup) side salads

Salad

3 cups kale, shredded
lemon juice
salt
3 cups spinach, torn
1 cup radicchio, shredded
2 cups baby beet leaves or red chard
3 cups red lettuce
1 cucumber
1 pomegranate
1 cup green grapes, halved
¼ cup pistachios
¼ cup hazelnuts
½ cup aged white cheddar cheese shreds

Note: Availability of salad leaves in winter can vary, so be prepared to improvise. It is important to include a mix of red (baby beet greens, such as "Bull's Blood," radicchio, red endive, red frisée, red oak leaf lettuce, red Swiss chard) and green leaves (arugula, bok choi, green endive, green frisée, green oak leaf lettuce, kale, mizuna, Romaine lettuce, spinach, tatsoi).

Rinse and dry the kale. First, tear out the big tough veins, leaving the sides of the leaves in large pieces. Mix together a splash of lemon juice and a generous pinch of salt. Massage the leaves with lemon and salt, squeezing and crushing them, to break down the fibers. Then press the leaves into a roll and use kitchen scissors to cut them into fine shreds. (Baby kale or microgreens do not need this tenderizing, but they are harder to find.) You need about 3 cups of shredded kale. Put them in a large mixing bowl.

Rinse and dry the spinach. Tear away the big veins. If the leaves are large, tear them into smaller pieces. You need about 3 cups of torn spinach. Add them to the large mixing bowl.

Remove any wilted outer leaves from the radicchio. Slice and chop the head until you have 1 cup of shreds. Add them to the large mixing bowl.

Add 2 cups of baby beet leaves or red chard and 3 cups of red lettuce to the large mixing bowl. Gently toss to mix all the leaves together.

Rinse and pat dry the cucumber. Dice it and put the bits in a small bowl.

Cut around the middle of the pomegranate, through the rind but not into the seeds. Gently pry it apart and work the peel off the segments, using the knife to separate segments if necessary. Remove all the red seeds and put them in a small bowl. Discard the white pith and rind.

Remove green grapes from the stem. Cut them in half. You need 1 cup of green grapes. Put them in a small bowl.

Measure ¼ cup pistachios and ¼ cup hazelnuts into a small bowl.

If you are using block cheese, shred it until you have ½ cup of aged white cheddar. However, it is easier to use pre-shredded cheese for salads because it doesn't cling to itself as much.

To assemble the salad, you need a large salad bowl or punch bowl. Put in enough leaves to cover the bottom. Then add a small amount of each topping. Cover with a handful or two of leaves, then add more toppings. Repeat this process until you have used all the leaves, ending with a layer of toppings. Building the salad this way, without tossing it, distributes the ingredients evenly so heavier ones don't fall to the bottom.

Dressing

zest of 1 lime
juice of 1 lime (about 2 tablespoons)
¼ teaspoon red peppercorns, crushed
¼ teaspoon Hawaiian jade green bamboo salt
½ teaspoon sweet marjoram flakes
a pinch of ground mustard
6 tablespoons full-flavored extra-virgin olive oil
1 tablespoon honey

You will need a container to make your salad dressing. Ideally, use a 6- to 8-ounce glass jar with a wide mouth and screw-on lid that will stay secure when shaken. You could also prepare the salad dressing in a mixing bowl if you prefer to blend it with a whisk or mixer.

Wash and pat dry the lime. Zest the lime into a small bowl. To mince the zest, you can either use scissors in a bowl, or a chef knife on a cutting board. You need flake-sized pieces that will distribute in the dressing.

Cut the lime in half. Juice the halves into the bowl of zest.

Measure ¼ teaspoon red peppercorns. Crush them in a mortar and pestle or a spice grinder. Add them to the bowl of lime juice.

Add ¼ teaspoon Hawaiian jade green bamboo salt, ½ teaspoon sweet marjoram flakes, and a pinch of ground mustard to the lime juice.

Pour the spiced lime juice into your salad dressing jar. Add 6 tablespoons full-flavored extra-virgin olive oil and 1 tablespoon honey. At this stage, the different liquids will float in separate layers. Close the jar tightly and shake until the salad dressing emulsifies. It should become a smooth, unified mass with a creamy yellowish color. If it starts to separate the moment you stop shaking, it's not done yet. Keep shaking until it holds together.

Winter Mint Tea

The tea is hot, but the herbs are cooling. They evoke the chill of winter. This soothes nerves and stomachs that may be overstimulated by the holidays.

Prep time: 5 minutes

Cooking time: about 10 minutes

Servings: 6

6 cups water

2 teaspoons dried peppermint

2 teaspoons dried spearmint

1 teaspoon dried raspberry leaf

½ teaspoon dried sage

¼ teaspoon pure wintergreen extract

Boil 6 cups water.

In a large teaball, put 2 teaspoons dried peppermint, 2 teaspoons dried spearmint, 1 teaspoon dried raspberry leaf, and ½ teaspoon dried sage. Steep for at least 5 minutes.

Remove teaball. Add ¼ teaspoon pure wintergreen extract and serve.

Crafty Crafts

Charlie Rainbow Wolf

YULE IS OFTEN THE time of year when those who haven't seen each other for a while make a special effort to try to get together. Fellowship and sharing are part of the festivities, and every culture has their own stories and traditions to share. It's a time for celebrating the return of the light; what better way to do this than with an activity to warm both the heart and the hearth?

When I lived in England, I spent many summer weekends traveling throughout the country working different folk festivals. On several occasions, I had the pleasure of engaging with Taffy Thomas, MBE, a Welsh folk story raconteur who wore an amazing coat. It was called his tale coat—and later spawned his book *Taffy's Coat Tales*. The tale coat is a truly remarkable garment, a long and flared cloak created by master artist Paddy Killer and depicting dozens of the stories Taffy told to his captivated audience.

The first time I saw Taffy was in an exhibition tent. A small child came up to him and pointed to a circular design on this coat and simply asked, "What's that?" Taffy burst into performance, leaving us all spellbound with one of his delightful tales.

Story Quilts

Story quilts fit nicely into Yuletide traditions for a myriad of reasons. Of course, the gift giving comes into it, as do the seasonal tales from around the world, but more than that, so does the fellowship. These quilts needn't be as elaborate as Taffy's tale coat, either!

One way to incorporate story quilting into Yuletide activities is to ask everyone to bring a scrap of fabric to make a friendship story quilt. These don't even have to be squares or pieces of themed fabric; there's such a thing called a "crazy quilt," where the abstract pieces of fabric are sewn in haphazard ways, and the only order to the design is at the edges, to get them straight.

Unlike Taffy's tale coat, this project does not have to be something that is worn. A story quilt is simply a quilt that tells a tale. It might be a careful selection of themed fabrics, or simply old scraps representational of something very personal. I have seen very simple nine-patch quilts tell the most compelling stories, the pattern on each small square representing a hobby, an activity, or an event from that person's life.

Materials

Fabric: This does not have to be expensive. Anything from old jeans or cotton shirts to purpose-bought themed fabric will work. It doesn't matter whether you are upcrafting something from an existing stash or buying something special, just ensure the quality is good.

Thread: Quilter's thread is the best; all-purpose thread will also work. Try to avoid the overly inexpensive thread as it tends to tangle and break.

Needles: These are called "sharps" and a packet with several sizes in it is not expensive; that way you can work out what seems to be the best fit for the project.

Cost: This is entirely up to you; scrap quilts made from items you have on hand could cost nothing more than time; if you purchase expensive fabric and a new sewing machine, then the cost will skyrocket.

Time spent: Anywhere from a few hours to several months, depending on the size of the quilt and how involved you want it to be.

Quilt Stories

I've had two story quilts in my life, and one is still in my possession some forty years later. It's a quilt that my late mother pieced together. In it's squares I see my old Job's Daughters bandana, the fabric of my Girl Scout dress, the material my maid of honor wore at my first wedding, a piece of my babysitter's dress, and so very much more. It's the story of my youth, my activities, and the neighbors around us, for some of their scraps went into the construction of the piece. I've tried to note what the fabric pieces are (without writing on the quilt of course) so that my daughter will understand what a treasure it has been when it eventually passes along to her.

The other story quilt I had was just as much of a story, but constructed very differently. Every piece measured a foot square, and it contained the names of my friends. They signed the fabric, and then I stitched over their names to quilt the front piece to the back piece.

My friend Debby did a different kind of story quilting. She took the themes from someone's life and cross-stitched them onto a large framed piece of aida (a special fabric for hand stitching) for the recipient to either hang as a framed piece of art or incorporate into a throw or other quilt. Her designs were caricatures of the people she was featuring—very entertaining, and beautiful at the same time.

Any of these would be suitable for the quilt project, as is resurrecting the idea of an autograph quilt, inviting everyone to either sign the fabric to be stitched later or to actually sew their own name onto something. To ensure everyone has something to take home with them, think smaller than an actual quilt; think quilted placemats or table runners. That way everyone could sign everyone else's fabric, and all attendees would have a keepsake.

If this is to be something worked on as a coven or a grove, consider a communal project. Everyone could bring their own piece to stitch, or—like the autograph quilt—it could be one large project that everyone works on simultaneously. Quilting bees of old were a wonderful time for socializing as well as for making the quilt! Think of it as a "year and a day" activity, started Yule this year and finished Yule next year. It could be a central table covering for future feasts or have some other group ritual use.

A story quilt does not have to be a group activity. If your spiritual practice is one of solitude, create a personal story quilt by including fabrics, designs, and stitches that mean something to you. It's very soothing to sit inside on a cold and dark night with a piece of needlework, contemplating your path and letting the fabric and stitches tell your tale.

Quilt fabric needn't be expensive. Any fabric works, providing it is structurally sound. If you choose the autograph quilt, bed sheets and batting—the filling between the layers that makes the actual warmth of the quilt—are easily obtainable from retailers online or in stores. To go a bit fancier with the theme, you might ask everyone to purchase a fat quarter (a quilter's measure of fabric) that means something special to them. One fat quarter would make several smaller pieces for the quilt.

My advice would be to keep things simple to start. A nine-patch square (think "tic-tac-toe" board) is one of the easiest and most common quilt patterns, and the patches can be put together in very attractive ways by clever use of color. Do a bit of research, and have some fun with this. After all, you're not just making a quilt, you're making a memory.

Further Reading

ScrapTherapy, The Versatile Nine Patch: 18 Fresh Designs for a Favorite Quilt Block by Joan Ford, 2017.

101 Nine Patch Quilts by Marti Michell, 1999.

Crazy Quilting: The Complete Guide by J. Marsha Michler 2008

How to Quilt: A Beginner's Guide to Learn How to Quilt Step-by-Step by Rebecca Wellner, 2018.

Taffy's Coat Tales: A Collection of Stories from Taffy Thomas, MBE, Laureate for Storytelling 2010–2012 by Taffy Thomas.

Candle Magic

Ember Grant

THIS IS THE LONGEST night of the year, but also the time when daylight grows steadily stronger in the days and weeks to come. Traditionally, at the Winter Solstice we celebrate the return of the sun. This ancient celebration, acknowledged by many cultures around the world, is often a time we draw close to one another to celebrate and renew peace, faith, and love.

Circle of Light

This ritual is for peace of all life and for Mother Earth. Choose an object for the center of your altar layout that represents life—a tree of life symbol, for example, or a photo of the earth. Surround this symbol with as many candles as you can gather—arrange them in a circle around it. It's actually best if you use different candles in a variety of sizes and colors because this represents the variety of beings on earth.

On each candle, write an expression you wish to evoke. For example: peace, love, kindness, forgiveness, understanding, acceptance, healing—anything you wish for our world, the planet, and all living things. If you wish, you can write these words on the bottom of the candle if it's big enough, or on the sides if using taper candles.

If you wish, decorate your altar with seasonal decorations such as pine, holly, and other evergreens or acorns and pine cones. Just be sure the plant materials don't get too close to the candles. You can use candleholders if that helps. You can add crystals to the arrangement as well.

When you're ready, visualize a divine, sacred, loving, and life-giving light—the light of life itself—embracing the entire world and every being in it. This light is filled with peace, healing, and love. As you light each candle, speak the word you've carved on it.

When all candles are lit, say:

> *Circle of light, embrace us all, children of Mother Earth.*
> *Circle of light, heal us all, including Mother Earth.*
> *Help us see that we are one.*
> *Unite us. Protect us.*
> *Circle of light, connect us.*
> *Blessed be.*

Since you may be using a variety of candle sizes, you don't need to allow them all to burn out. Instead, burn them as long as you wish and then snuff them out. Repeat the ritual as often as you wish until all the candles have been spent.

Year and a Day Resolution Spell

In ancient Rome, in 46 BCE, Julius Caesar wanted the new year to begin on the day after the Winter Solstice. It makes sense to have the new year begin as the days begin to lengthen. But because the "rules" at the time dictated that the new year begin on the day of the new moon, that didn't happen (Frederich-Mueller 2020, 182). Despite the fact that our new year celebration is about a week after the solstice, we still approach the new year with a sense of renewal, often seeking a new outlook and planning to make change. To that end, make a traditional New Year's resolution and perform this ritual on the day after the Winter Solstice.

This spell could get messy depending on how comfortable you are working with hot wax, so be sure you have an appropriate place to work. Use a red or white candle; a taper works best. Anoint the candle as you choose and create your sacred space.

Write about your hopes and dreams for the year ahead. You can also express your fears and concerns. Write down goals you have and things you hope to accomplish. Write secrets too—things you may not want to express to others. Use magical intent to overcome obstacles and achieve goals. As you write them, see them becoming reality; see your fears diminishing.

Fold the paper, place it in an envelope, and seal it with wax. If you have a formal seal, you can use that, but if you don't, that's fine. Just drop some wax on the envelope flap. After adding the wax, speak these words:

Keep these words and wishes well—
with this wax I seal the spell.

Let the wax dry. Do not break the seal for a year and a day. Keep your goals in mind, but don't obsess over them. Put a reminder in your calendar to open it, but hide the envelope until then and try to forget about it. Allow the candle to burn out. When you do open the envelope, revisit your feelings and reflect on the previous year.

Yuletide Hearth Blessing

If you don't have a fireplace or wood-burning stove, this ritual can be done using an outdoor firepit. If you don't have any of these items, use a heatproof dish to symbolize the hearth. If possible, perform this ritual as close to the solstice as possible—ideally on the longest night.

Gather seasonal decorations based on what you have accessible. Depending on where you live, look for acorns, cones from conifer trees, or other nuts and seeds. Also obtain 3–5 evergreen branches such as pine, cedar, or holly. You can purchase these if you don't have a place to gather them. Be sure you choose a branch size appropriate to your hearth space. If you're just using a heatproof dish or cauldron, you'll need smaller branches. The final thing you'll need is a red candle of any size.

Arrange the candle, branches, seeds, cones, nuts, etc. around your cauldron or place them on or near the hearth (but not too close to the candle or the fire). If you have a mantle over your fireplace, or even just a mantel shelf, decorate that area. If you're using a smaller container, find a safe place for it, a place where you can leave it for about a week.

Light a fire and the red candle; alternately, just burn a red candle in the container you selected. Be careful that the branches aren't too close to the flame. You can incorporate a Yule log into the ritual if you wish. After the arrangement is in place and the fire has been lit, speak these words:

> *Bless this hearth,*
> *may it bring*
> *a wonderful year to come.*
> *Bless this home*
> *as we await*
> *the returning of the sun.*

Allow both the fire and red candle to burn out. Discard the wax. Remove the plant materials after the first of the year and toss out the seeds and nuts for wildlife; bury the branches.

Reference
Frederich-Mueller, Hans. *The Pagan World: Ancient Religions Before Christianity*. The Great Courses/The Teaching Company. Chantilly, Virginia, 2020.

Yule Ritual

Tess Whitehurst

YULE IS CHARACTERIZED BY polarity: celebration and introspection, endings and beginnings, the blinding brightness of snow sparkling in sunshine and the silent darkness of the year's longest night. Similarly, when it comes to clearing and blessing the home in the days leading up to Yule, two contrasting intentions intertwine. The middle of winter guides us to create a safe haven for stillness and rest, while the forthcoming rebirth of the sun inspires us to welcome in the expansive, energizing forces the solstice is about to usher in.

Cleansing and Blessing the Home at Midwinter

This ritual incorporates both intentions, with the added benefit of harmonizing the polarities within you, your household, and your home in order to promote inner balance and serenity, and to steady you for a healthy, wealthy, and successful new cycle ahead. It will also break up any stuck or heavy energy that may have accumulated during the winter season and transmute it into happiness, positivity, and luck.

First, clear your home of unwanted items. Either place them in a trash or recycling bin or, if they're reusable, get them ready to donate or sell.

Then take some time to tidy, organize, and clean. If weather permits, also sweep your doorstep and wash your front door, first inside, then out. (Dunking a clean rag in a bucket of warm water with a few drops of essential oil of spearmint is my favorite way to do this. Cedar, sage, peppermint, and rosemary are also good choices. But if your skin is sensitive to essential oils, either use plain water or wear rubber gloves.)

Once your home is physically clean and clear, you'll be ready to perform the following ritual.

Supplies

Sleigh bells
1 stick woodsy incense like cedar, pine, frankincense, or juniper
1 stick sweet or spicy incense like cinnamon, vanilla, or clove
A dish or a plate
A lighter or matches
Sunflower oil (for cooking)

Assemble all ingredients on your altar or in a central or significant location in your home, such as a counter, table, or stove. (Anywhere that feels right to you will work.)

Stand or sit before the ingredients. Take some deep breaths and hold your hands in prayer pose as you relax your body and center your mind.

Say:

> *Ancient Mother, Glorious God,*
> *Womb of Creation and Creation Itself,*
> *Deepest Darkness, Brightest Light,*
> *I call on you now to watch over this working.*
> *Thank you for helping me create clear and sacred space in my home,*
> *For relaxation and for rest,*

For safety and protection,
For health and wellness,
And to usher in beauty, brilliance, abundance, and the light.
I now perform this clearing and blessing ceremony for my highest
and truest good, and the highest and truest good of all.
Ancient Mother, Glorious God,
I call on you.
I honor you.
I invite you in.
Thank you.
Hail and welcome.

If weather permits, open your windows at least a crack. And if you don't have pets or small children who may run out, open the doors as well.

Pick up the sleigh bells. Open your front door wide and shake the sleigh bells within the threshold. Close the door (or leave it open a crack) and begin moving in a counterclockwise direction through each room and area of your space while shaking the sleigh bells. This will raise the vibration and get formerly stuck energy moving.

Set the sleigh bells back down and light the woodsy incense. While holding the dish or plate beneath the incense to catch ash and burning embers, retrace your footsteps: begin at your front door and open it wide. Cleanse the threshold with smoke. Shut the door (or leave it open a crack) and move through each room and area in a counterclockwise direction while cleansing the space with smoke. This will create a portal of light and positivity while transforming any remaining challenging energy into positivity. Safely extinguish the incense.

Next, light the sweet or spicy incense. While holding the dish or plate under it, return to your front door and open it wide. Cleanse the threshold with smoke. Close your door (or leave it open a crack) and cleanse your home with smoke while moving through each room and area of your home in a clockwise direction this time. This will invite in sweetness, abundance, and luck while further raising the vibration in your home. Safely extinguish the incense.

Now pour a little bit of sunflower oil on the dish or plate. (It's okay if it mixes with ash from the incense.) Return to your front door, but stand outside this time. Close your door and use the oil to trace a small five-pointed star (pentagram) on your door to seal in positivity and spiritually protect your home. Repeat with any additional doors that open to the outside. (You can approach them from the outside of your home or the inside, but make sure to anoint them on the outside. Also keep in mind that it's ideal if you go from one door to another in a clockwise direction.)

Close any windows that you have opened.

Now, return to the location where you began the ritual. Once again, hold your hands in prayer pose. Breathe deeply, relax, and center your mind. Feel rooted into the earth and connected with the cosmos. Envision a sphere of golden light completely filling and encompassing your home like a cocoon. See and sense it gently rotating in a clockwise direction to seal in the energy and further promote positivity and protection.

Say:

Ancient Mother, Glorious God,
Womb of Creation and Creation Itself,
Deepest Darkness, Brightest Light,
You have supported me in consecrating this space.
I dedicate it to you with love.
May it be a sacred temple of peace, serenity, and healing.
May it be a portal that brings forth wealth, abundance,
and success.
May all who live here prosper and thrive.
Thank you, thank you, thank you.
Blessed be.
And so it is.

Lie down on the floor (or a couch or bed if that's not comfortable) to release any extra energy you may have called into your field and to reconnect to the earth. Then have at least a little bit to eat or drink to recharge and ground your energy.

Dispose of any remaining sunflower oil, hang the sleigh bells on or over the front door, and feel free to burn the remainder of the incense at any point throughout the Yule season.

Notes

Notes

Notes

Imbolc

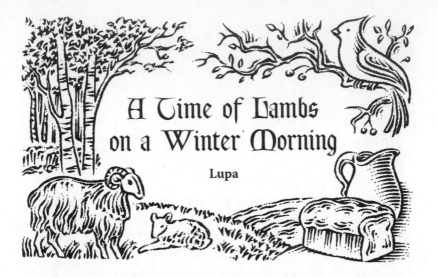

A Time of Lambs on a Winter Morning

Lupa

IT IS A CHILLY late January morning. The sun is a pale glow behind a haze of soft gray clouds and a hint of mist, just hovering over the tops of the shore pines. Bundled in sweats, barn coat, and rubber boots, I crunch my way down the damp gravel driveway toward the barn. I can already hear the chickens muttering in the coop, the younger ones laying eggs in spite of the season, and further off, the sheep call out for their breakfast.

As I walk to the back of the barn to where the flock impatiently bleats, in the corner I see one of the ewes standing over a trio of freshly born lambs. Two are already struggling to stand and nurse; she nuzzles them encouragingly and makes low, gentle sounds that they answer with their own insistent calls. The third lamb lies motionless in the straw. Upon closer inspection I find no heartbeat; unsurprising since the poor little thing hadn't even been able to struggle out of its caul.

No time to mourn, though. The wind is picking up a bit as the sun starts to warm the air. Mama Ewe doesn't want to head into the nice, cozy stall I have set up for her, but I pick up her lambs and place them in the deep, dry layer of straw and coax her in with them while keeping the rest of the flock from piling in on top of us.

(No easy feat, that.) Once set up with a heat lamp in the corner and plenty of food and water, I leave them to settle in, then go to attend to the last triplet.

It's not uncommon for one of a set of triplets or quadruplets to not make it. Even though St. Croix sheep are a hardy breed and generally need little help with lambing, sheep in general have a whole host of things that can go wrong with them during pregnancy and labor. Some of these are caused by infectious diseases, but even in an otherwise healthy flock, a stillborn lamb, or one that dies shortly after birth, may result from the ewe having a lack of a particular nutrient during pregnancy, a difficult birth process, a congenital defect, or even being an inexperienced mother who doesn't know how to care for her new young. Previous testing ruled out disease in the flock, and we've bulked up their feed, so it's anyone's guess what happened.

I bundle up the lamb in an empty feed sack and carry it out to the woods beyond the last pasture. There's a little clearing among the pines where I lay the remains out upon dead wet grass and dried blackberry brambles. There are plenty of hungry scavengers who will appreciate this meal: crows and ravens, coyotes, maybe even a black bear taking a quick break from hibernation in our relatively mild winter. Nothing goes to waste here, and now my attention needs to be on the surviving twins, making sure that they're getting their first good meal of colostrum.

No fear there. This is an experienced ewe, and by the time I've gotten back to the barn to clean the lambs' umbilical stumps and make sure they're all dried off, Mama Ewe has already gotten them both to nurse heartily. They'll spend the next few days in here to bond and let the lambs grow stronger, and then go back out with the herd so I can clean the stall for the next new arrivals (who will only show up when they're darned good and ready.)

This is how I have spent my past few Imbolcs. I moved to a farm owned by a couple of friends of mine to be the on-site caretaker for the various and sundry animals, since they still work back in the city. The sheep are theirs, while I have my own flock of chickens, and we recently added a nice collection of geese and ducks to keep the grass mowed down in the orchard. One of my friends maintains an ever-growing nursery full of native plants, many of which have been dispersed throughout the farm's more open areas to encourage overall biodiversity.

I grew up in a rural area but spent over a decade living in cities before landing here on the farm. It's the first time that, as a Pagan, I've been living a truly agricultural life. And it's brought the Wheel of the Year into sharper focus. Most Pagans these days live in cities, and the crop-and-livestock-related imagery of the sabbats is theoretical at best for a lot of us. It doesn't make our rites any less valid, but I know I'm not the only Pagan who's sometimes found it a little harder to connect with Imbolc than, say, Samhain.

No one should be surprised, then, that it took caring for actual, living sheep for me to find a real, personal anchor for this holiday. Previously, Imbolc was just the time after Yule's festivities when the Pacific Northwest's winters got even wetter and grayer, and I might light a candle now and then to remind myself that it wouldn't be too terribly long before spring started pushing the crocuses up. But remember that Imbolc (or Oimelc) means "belly of the mother" or "ewe's milk," referring to the lamb-heavy ewes whose udders are swollen with life-giving milk. Now, I looked forward to when they would bring forth the lambs they'd been carrying for almost half a year.

Here's the thing, though. Just as Imbolc isn't yet spring, but the middle of winter, so lambing season isn't just a time for bouncy new babies. It's also a reminder that the death we normally focus on during Samhain is still very much a part of the life cycle, and the cruel chill of this time can cut short the newest lives. And while I may mourn the loss of a lamb or two each season, I can't stop to do my grieving. Instead, I work through those emotions as I lay out the lifeless remains in the scavengers' feasting forest and make sure the rest of the flock is well-fed and cared for.

There's something comforting about the press of warm, living sheep against me as I bring their daily hay and grain out to them. Like a lot of people, I used to think of sheep as dumb domestic animals that had all the smarts bred out of them to make them more pliable. And sure, selective breeding has enhanced a sheep's herding instinct and made them more docile around humans. Perhaps I'm a little biased because St. Croix are a particularly "goaty" sort of hair sheep breed, but I no longer see sheep as unintelligent. This little flock of less than ten adults and assorted lambs has a ton of personality. They're bold when it comes to demanding food (no matter how much they get to eat each day), and even willful when I try to move them from one pasture to another and they find something tasty along the way. They're not especially interested in being petted, but they'll happily take treats. For this flock, at least, food is a love language.

The (thankfully hornless) ram is a bit of a jerk who will try to sneak up and butt you from behind if you aren't careful, but we've reached an understanding that if he doesn't come after me, I won't then proceed to chase him all over the field to let him know just how displeased I am about the matter. A quick stomp in his direction and he backs down with little fuss. For a while he had an accomplice; one of our old-lady ewes decided she was going to get in on the butting fun, and they became quite the tag team. Sadly, we lost her to various old age ailments a while back, and I think he and I both miss her.

You're more likely to find Pagans who work with the archetypal animal spirits of wildlife rather than those of domestic species. (These are what are often referred to as "totems." I've chosen a more culturally generic term as a way of moving away from appropriation.) Those who do ask domestic spirits for help usually gravitate toward the more charismatic ones like Dog and Horse. The spirits of "food" species like Sheep, Chicken and Cow are less considered. Oh, sure, sometimes we might use the imagery of cattle at harvest time, like driving the herd between two fires to help them get through the winter. But how many Pagans have ever interacted with cattle in a more personal manner than a cheeseburger?

I've spent over a decade working with the archetypal animal spirits of those species that most of us only ever meet on a dinner plate, from Chicken to Dungeness Crab. Overwhelmingly I've found that they feel overlooked compared to their more venerated wild counterparts, with none of the romance and glory we give to Wolf, Stag, Eagle, and so forth. This isn't surprising given how divorced many of us are from the sources of our food, and how we often split wild animals and domestic animals into a "good wilderness" and "bad agriculture" dichotomy. I'm of the firm belief that we really need to dismantle factory farming and go back to more sustainable ways of raising animals for meat (as well as eat less meat, but that's a whole different article). But the current state of things is not the fault of the animals, nor their overarching spirits.

So my connection to a more meaningful Imbolc has also tied into that need to raise up our relationships to the domestic animals we all too often take for granted. If Samhain is all about the bats, cats and, yes, sacred cattle, then Imbolc's animals should include sheep of all sorts. Not only is it shifting the focus more firmly to the agricultural roots of this festival, but it's also giving us a chance to appreciate an animal that we often only think of as fluffy scenery on country drives.

I'm also more inclined to see Imbolc as a celebration of survival and savvy. You don't go and have your young out in the middle of a winter storm unless you have a decent chance of keeping them safe and warm until spring. And while many sheep may get to give birth, or at least bond with their lambs, in a nice indoor setting, most of them are perfectly capable of doing so outside. After all, shepherds have spent millennia tending to large flocks who never spent a day in any more substantial shelter than a copse of trees.

Finally, it is a time to appreciate everything in the world on its own terms. The cold gray days of mid-winter may not be my favorite, but they are blessedly quiet. And they're necessary for many beings in this temperate region to have a chance to rest, whether it's the trees readying themselves for spring's flowers or the bears a-snooze in their dens. It's a quiet time for work as well, for the nursery doesn't need watering and I don't have much in the way of out-of-town obligations, so I have many long stretches of days where I barely leave the comfort of the farm. This is a gift, and I need to remember that.

In the same way, I am better able to appreciate the spirit Sheep as a guide, whose first lesson to me was to cast aside my biases and let the beings, places, and things I encounter tell me who they are themselves. So it is that now Imbolc is not just a time for me to look forward to a new crop of lambs to welcome into the world, but also to reflect on how I may make myself more open to the world as the year unfolds.

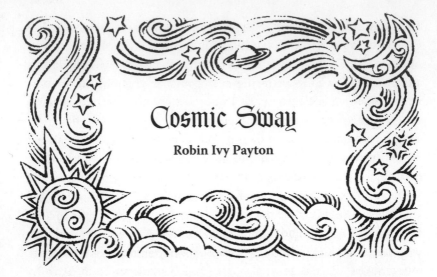

Cosmic Sway

Robin Ivy Payton

DAYLIGHT IS LENGTHENING, the Sun grows stronger, and February dawns with Imbolc. February 2 is also known as Groundhog Day when the groundhog's shadow, or lack thereof, determines the length of winter. This nonscientific tradition plays into the element of light and the Sun's increasing power. In the Wheel of the Year, this is the childhood phase of the Sun. The ewe begins to milk for her babies. The ground warms, and early sprouts emerge. In some zones, there are winter thaws and surprisingly spring-like days. Like Aquarius's element, air, this is a time of cleansing and refreshing. The New Moon closest to Imbolc brings Chinese New Year, a traditional time for thorough cleaning and "sweeping away of dust." Chinese Year of the Tiger begins on February 1, the eve of Aquarius New Moon.

Astrology for Imbolc

New Moon in Aquarius arrives with Imbolc on February 1, 2022, which is also Chinese New Year. Sweep out the cobwebs physically and otherwise. Remove obstacles for this cycle of strong beginnings and long-term actions. Aquarius Moon favors commitments, and Saturn nearby adds serious intent. Planet Uranus in Taurus aligns with the Sun and Moon, inspiring reinvention. Some will make radical change with this aspect, which brings out the inner rebel. Mercury, Venus, and Mars are in Capricorn, helping with goals and step-by-step plans. Mercury is retrograde, however, until Friday, February 3. Legal contracts or important announcements may be best initiated after that date.

Also note the first two days of February share a void-of-course Moon from 6:01 a.m. to 5:59 a.m. EST the next day. This makes February 1 a particularly good vacation or celebration time. Personal and business matters that require negotiations or judgment calls may be better timed a few days later, as Mercury moves direct.

Sync body and mind with the return of light through a regular practice of Sun salutations. Like creatures of the earth who stir from hibernation, we emerge from conservation mode and benefit from movement. Alternately, if it's been a busy or tiring winter, begin with gentle stretching and extra immune support before trying more invigorating exercise. Paired with either salutations or yin postures, yogic breathing helps calm the nervous system, ruled by the sign Aquarius. Group classes and practices, whether virtual or in person, provide social interaction and participation as the Sun travels this sign related to collective energy, friendship, and community.

February Full Moon

On February 14, the Moon enters Leo at 6:17 a.m. EST, and on February 16 the Moon is Full in this heart-centered sign. Make art, music, and homemade valentines under creative Leo Moon. Performances such as plays or concerts make excellent Valentine's dates since Leo rules the stage. Generosity and fun are enhanced as the Moon warms up in Leo, then peaks on February 16 at 11:56 a.m. Just hours before, the Moon and Saturn are opposite. Be objective with serious decisions or considerations. Temperance and courage are called for, and as the Moon opposes the Sun directly, positive outcomes are favored. The Moon is void of course from 11:56 a.m.

to 3:41 p.m. EST, then crosses into Virgo. Take a little time for self-care or leisure while the Moon is void of course.

Astrological Spirits and Symbols

Infuse your seasonal spells with astrological magic. For Imbolc, combine the Star card with others that illustrate your dreams. The Star depicts an Aquarian-like water bearer and offers flow between the present and future. Temperance represents spiritual guidance and also shows water pouring between containers, like blending the earthly and heavenly. Surround these hopeful images with others of your liking: cups for emotions and love, pentacles for earth and abundance. Wands cards signify the fire element, like this month's Leo Moon. Swords relate to air qualities, like Aquarius, our current Sun sign.

Amethyst stone aligns beautifully with Aquarius New Moon. Place some by the bed or in your workspace to release habits or addictions and to stay on a positive course. Clear quartz signifies clearing for what's to come. For Full Moon in Leo, use crystals for the heart including green aventurine, fluorite, or malachite for balancing emotions. All month long, wear or display turquoise stones, which offer Aquarian qualities like hope, intuition, and friendship. In your rituals, call upon animal spirits with Aquarius nature. Owl sees the broader view, is patient, observant, and objective. Invoke the owl's energy for wisdom and good judgment.

At Full Moon time, Lion and Peacock embody traits of both Aquarius and Leo, this month's solar-lunar polarity. For courage and heart, call on the lion, a symbol of the strengthening Sun. Lioness both hunts and raises the young, and is therefore a strong spirit for women and for grounding in feminine greatness. Peacock blends Aquarius's vision with Leo's expressive traits. Its iridescent feathers contain the shapes of eyes, symbolic of knowing and sight. One of this bird's power cycles is spring, the season just ahead. Peacock is associated with integrity and resilience. And, naturally, the male's incredible colors draw our admiration. To attract positive attention or re-instill hopefulness, invite Peacock's spiritual guidance between Imbolc and Full Moon.

Finally, note that Year of the Water Tiger begins with Imbolc and Chinese New Year, as they arrive simultaneously this year. Associated with both New and Full Moons, the tiger is a spirit of devotion and adventure. Call upon the tiger to renew vitality and passion in your life. Unlike many animal spirits, this cat relates to all directions and all elements according to type and color (Andrews 1993, 319). With Tiger spirit, reflect on the speed of life's events. Tiger can run at top speed, but only for short distances. On the hunt, they move slowly and quietly, in the nighttime, under the Moon. Tiger may appear or be invoked for awareness of pace, stamina, and visibility as you move through late winter.

Reference

Andrews, Ted. *Animal Speak: The Spiritual & Magical Powers of Creatures Great & Small.* St. Paul, MN: Llewellyn Publications, 1993.

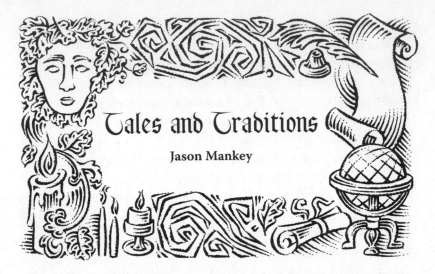

Tales and Traditions

Jason Mankey

OVER THE LAST FEW decades, modern Witches have used a variety of names for the holiday most of us today call Imbolc. Some of the earliest Witches called the holiday "February Eve" and celebrated on the last night of January. Other Witches used the name "Candlemas," a Christian holiday celebrated on February 2. In the Reclaiming Tradition of Witchcraft, Imbolc is often called Brigid, the name of one of Celtic Ireland's most famous goddesses and one of Catholic Ireland's most famous saints.

Imbolc: The Many Faces of Brigid

In my personal practice, I revere Brigid as the "goddess who has always been there." When Ireland went from Celtic Paganism to Catholic-style Christianity, out of all the deities in Ireland, it was Brigid who transitioned mostly intact from the old religion to the new (and she even got to keep her name). Later, Brigid's name would be found in New Orleans Voodoo and Haitian Vodou as Maman Brigitte. There are a handful of ancient Pagan deities who have been absorbed into other religions, but Brigid has probably accomplished that more successfully than any other one.

Brigid is often referred to as a "Celtic goddess" but it's more honest to say that she was an "Irish-Celtic goddess." Just how far her worship extended over Ireland and the rest of the British Isles is an open question. There are some scholars that believe Brigid's worship was limited to the area around Ireland's County Kildare while others believe her worship was more far flung. The Romano-British goddess Brigantia is believed by some to be a version of Ireland's Brigit (Hutton 1996, 135). That doesn't quite make Brigid a universal Celtic deity, but it does extend her reach a long way.

Among the Irish-Celts, Brigid was a goddess of learning, prophecy, poetry, healing, and metalwork. Her association with metalwork and the forge, along with her name, might also indicate that she was a fire goddess. Brigid actually translates as "fiery arrow," again linking her to fire and also perhaps to war (Hutton 1996, 135). This makes her similar to the Greek goddess Athena (Roman Minerva) who ruled over a similar set of attributes. In Irish mythology, Brigid is the daughter of the Dagda, one of the kings of the Tuatha Dé Danann, the gods of Celtic Ireland.

The myths involving the Catholic Saint Brigid are extremely varied. In some versions, she acts as a wet-nurse to the baby Jesus, and in other tales Brigid is a reformed Druidess who converted to Christianity and became a nun. Complicating things even further is a medieval Irish manuscript that lists over twenty-five different Brigids in Irish history (Hutton, 1993, 153)! It's possible that one of these twenty-five different Brigids was an actual flesh and blood human being, but that real person was absorbed by the goddess Brigid. The idea that many Christian saints are transformed versions of ancient Pagan deities is often overstated, but in the case of Brigid, it is undoubtedly true.

Much of what we know about the goddess Brigid is directly related to what we know about the Christian saint of the same name, and the mythology and worship of the two figures is very much intertwined. Kildare Abbey is home to a sacred flame in honor of Saint Brigid, but it's likely the fire kept at the abbey dates back to the worship of the goddess Brigid. Also interesting is the name of Kildare itself. Kildare translates as "Church of the Oak Tree," hinting at more Pagan roots. The oak was not generally revered among Christians, making it unlikely for the namesake of a church. Sacred flames kept burning for over one-thousand years are also rare in Christian practice, making it far more likely that the custom was inherited from the Pagans of Celtic Ireland (Weber 2015, 11).

Many of the customs and symbols associated with Saint Brigid have become commonplace among Witches. Brigid's Cross, generally consisting of four arms of equal length and a square in the middle, is commonly seen on drawings and statues featuring the goddess Brigid. While many believe Brigid's Cross to be a Pagan survival, its origin is probably a Christian one, and in this case represents Witches borrowing from Catholics. Also probably a Christian tradition is Brigid's Bed, a custom featuring a small handmade "bed" in which lies a corn dolly adorned with ribbons and other decorative items to represent Saint Brigid. In some parts of Ireland, Brigid's Bed was taken door to door on the night of January 31 (Brigid's Eve) in a way similar to trick or treating on Halloween.

Saint Brigid's feast day is on February 1, the same day most Witches celebrate Imbolc. This suggests that Imbolc was probably sacred to the goddess of the same name as well. It's believed that the word Imbolc has something to do with milk, and here the traits of the saint might lead us to a better understanding of the goddess. Saint Brigid was considered a friend and healer of animals, especially of livestock, and as a giver of grain. If the goddess Brigid is connected to the Celtic-Pagan celebration of Imbolc, it's likely that the deity Brigid was seen as a goddess of animals by the Pagans of Ireland.

The cult of Brigid the goddess has spread far from Ireland and Christendom and can even be found in the Afro-Caribbean religions of Haitian Vodou and New Orleans Voodoo. There, Maman Brigitte (or Brijit) is the wife of Baron Samedi and is honored as one of the *loa* (spirits that intercede with the divine for humans) alongside her husband. (Alternatively, Maman Brigitte is sometimes also known as Mademoiselle Brigette and Gran Brigitte.) Both Maman Brigitte and Baron Samedi are Les Gede loa, meaning they are seen as loa of the dead. Both Maman Brigitte and Baron Samedi are traditionally honored as the first woman and first man buried at every cemetery (Dorsey 2005, 41–42).

While it's commonly accepted that Maman Brigitte is somehow reflective of Brigid of Ireland, there is some disagreement. Interestingly, some Vodou lineages in Haiti sing a song about "Manman Brijit who came from England," which suggests a link between the loa and the saint and goddess named Brigid. It's common for the loa to each be associated with a Catholic saint, and it would make sense if Maman Brigitte was represented as Saint Brigid, but instead she's more likely to be represented by the Italian Saint Rosalia (Tann 2016, 120). What's not in doubt is just how powerful Brigid remains in the modern world in a variety of traditions.

References

Dorsey, Lilith. *Voodoo and Afro-Caribbean Paganism*. New York: Citadel Press, 2005.

Hutton, Ronald. *The Pagan Religions of the Ancient British Isles*. Oxford: Blackwell Publishers, 1993.

———. *The Stations of the Sun: A History of the Ritual Year in Britain*. Oxford: Oxford University Press, 1996.

Tann, Mambo Chita. *Haitian Vodou: An Introduction to Haiti's Indigenous Spiritual Tradition*. Woodbury MN: Llewellyn Publications, 2016.

Weber, Courtney. Brigid: *History, Mystery, and Magick of the Celtic Goddess*. San Francisco, CA: Weiser Books, 2015.

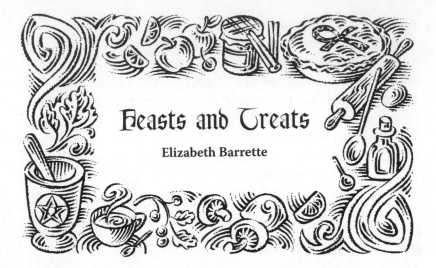

Feasts and Treats

Elizabeth Barrette

IMBOLC CELEBRATES THE FIRST signs of the sun's return and the coming spring. Winter is winding down, but the warmth and life have not yet returned. So this holiday focuses on hope for the future and brighter days to come.

Citrus Chicken

This recipe uses citrus fruits, many of which peak in winter due to growing in warm climates with a different seasonal cycle than temperate regions. Citrus fruits with red, orange, or yellow colors represent the sun. If you wish to include limes or other green citrus, their color can stand for the spring buds soon to emerge.

The other ingredients, such as chicken and dried herbs, are readily available all year round. Chicken represents the abundance ahead. In our coven, we enjoy making chicken because some people like meat but not everyone wants red meat. Herbs bring a magic of their own as well.

Prep time: 20 minutes
Cooking time: 60–100 minutes
Servings: 4–6

At least 6 assorted citrus fruits (such as 3 oranges and 3 lemons)
1 inch of fresh ginger root (about 1 tablespoon grated)
¼ teaspoon pink salt
½ teaspoon mixed pepper (black, white, green, pink)
1 teaspoon sweet basil flakes
1 teaspoon sweet marjoram flakes
1 whole chicken (4–5 pounds)
½ teaspoon tapioca starch
cotton kitchen twine

Preheat the oven at 350°F for at least 10 minutes. Coat a roasting pan with cooking spray. Add a roasting rack if you have one.

Zest two different citrus fruits, such as an orange and a lemon, into a small bowl. After removing the zest, cut them in half and squeeze the juice until you have at least ¼ cup of juice. It's okay if that includes some pulp. Combine the juice and the zest.

Peel a 1-inch chunk of fresh ginger root, then grate it; you should get about 1 tablespoon. Add the grated ginger to the citrus juice.

To the bowl of citrus juice, add ¼ teaspoon pink salt, ½ teaspoon mixed pepper (black, white, green, pink), 1 teaspoon sweet basil flakes, and 1 teaspoon sweet marjoram flakes. Stir the juice to combine the ingredients. Then stir in ½ teaspoon tapioca starch until dissolved.

Remove the giblets from the chicken and set them aside; they are not needed for this recipe. Rinse the chicken and pat it dry.

Quarter two different citrus fruits, such as an orange and a lemon. Stuff the cavity of the chicken with as many quarters as will fit; usually you can get one into the neck hole too. Use cotton kitchen twine to tie the ends of the drumsticks together, which holds the cavity closed. Pin the neck hole with a toothpick if necessary. Place the chicken breast-side up in the roasting pan. If there are citrus quarters left over from stuffing the cavity, tuck them around the chicken in the bottom of the pan. Using a pastry brush, cover the chicken with the citrus juice blend.

Put the chicken in the oven. Roast the chicken at 350°F for 15–20 minutes per pound; larger birds take longer. If the skin gets too dark, then cover the chicken with a tent of aluminum foil to minimize further browning. The chicken is done when a meat thermometer reads 165°F, the skin is golden-brown, and the juices run clear. There should be no pink showing when the meat is cut open.

Remove the chicken from the oven. Transfer it from the roasting pan to a serving platter. Take off the twine from the drumsticks. Allow the chicken to rest for at least 5 minutes before serving.

While the chicken is resting, cut at least two different citrus fruits into slices about ⅛ to ¼ inch thick. Arrange a ring of citrus slices in alternating colors around the chicken.

Goat/Sheep Cheese Dip

Imbolc is the time when the spring births begin. Goats have kids and sheep have lambs. So the mothers, previously dried off for the winter, begin to give milk again. This milk is used for many purposes, including the production of soft fresh cheese. The following recipe capitalizes on this seasonal resource.

Prep time: 10 minutes
Servings: 8–10

zest and juice of half a lemon (about 1½ tablespoons juice)
8 ounces soft goat or sheep cheese
¼ cup full-flavor extra-virgin olive oil
¼ cup plain yogurt
2 tablespoons snipped fresh Italian parsley
1 tablespoon snipped fresh basil
½ teaspoon snipped fresh thyme
½ teaspoon snipped fresh rosemary
¼ teaspoon sea salt
¼ teaspoon black pepper
pita chips or fresh vegetable spears

Collect the zest and juice of half a lemon, about 1½ tablespoons juice, and put that in a blender or food processor.

Add 8 ounces soft goat or sheep cheese, ¼ cup full-flavor extra-virgin olive oil, and ¼ cup plain yogurt.

Blend until smooth. Scrape the cheese blend into a small bowl.

Use kitchen scissors to cut the fresh herbs into small bits. You need 2 tablespoons snipped fresh Italian parsley, 1 tablespoon snipped fresh basil, ½ teaspoon snipped fresh thyme, and ½ teaspoon snipped fresh rosemary. Add those to the cheese blend.

Add ¼ teaspoon sea salt and ¼ teaspoon black pepper to the cheese blend. Stir in the seasonings until combined.

Serve the cheese dip with pita chips or fresh vegetable spears.

White Hot Chocolate

In the coldest part of winter, when all the world is white, it's nice to settle down with a hot drink. This variation on hot chocolate uses white chocolate instead of milk chocolate for a subtle and creamy treat. Spices bring out the floral notes.

Prep time: 5 minutes
Cooking time: 5–10 minutes
Servings: 8

8 cups whole milk
2 cups gourmet white chocolate, chopped
1 teaspoon pure vanilla extract
1 vanilla bean
½ teaspoon cardamom

Pour 8 cups whole milk into a saucepan and turn on low heat. Be careful to simmer, not boil, to avoid forming a skin.

This recipe calls for real white chocolate made with cocoa butter, and if it contains vanilla, that should also be genuine and not artificial, hence gourmet. Chop it and measure 2 cups, then add that to the warming milk. Whisk gently until the chocolate melts into the milk.

Add 1 teaspoon pure vanilla extract. Cut the vanilla bean in half the long way, scrape out the insides, then add the insides and outsides to the milk. Stir in ½ teaspoon cardamom.

Heat the white hot chocolate until it steams gently. Remove the vanilla bean shell. Carefully pour the white hot chocolate into 8 mugs and serve.

Crafty Crafts

Charlie Rainbow Wolf

TO ME, IMBOLC MARKS the first days of spring. It is traditionally a time when the first of the season's lambs are starting to be born, when the first of the snowdrops are peeking their heads through the still chilly soil, and when—as the nights start to get ever lighter—the first tasks of spring cleaning are started. In fact, the original word *imbolg* actually means "sac" or "bag," while the old Irish word *oimelc* means "the milk of a ewe" ("Imbolc"). This definition only goes to enhance Imbolc as being the festival welcoming new life and plenty.

Imbolc is Brigid's festival. Before Saint Brigid became one of the main patron saints of Ireland, she was known as the goddess of healing and poetry. She is believed to bring fertility back to the land—and with spring starting to emerge during the time of her festival, it is easy to understand why!

Homage to Brigid is often paid by making a Saint Brigid's Cross. This was traditionally woven out of rushes, but in modern days yarn is frequently used. It's thought to keep bad luck away from the household where it is hung. There are many stories about its origin, but the actual cross is now a familiar emblem of both Brigid—the goddess or the saint—and Ireland.

Spindle Spinning

Even though spring is springing, the warmer weather has not yet arrived and the nights are still long and dark. Needlework in the form of mending or knitting was done by both men and women in the fishing town where I used to live—in fact, knitting was considered men's work until around the eighteenth century! The relationship between the fleece and the finished garment was much closer then, before yarn could easily be obtained by mail order or in a specialty shop with a large selection. The sheep had to be shorn and then the fleece had to be washed and carded—a way of combing it with special tools—before it could be spun.

You don't have to do all of that though (although having done it myself, it is very interesting to do it just once so you really get to know the yarn). It's much more convenient to buy ready-to-spin fleece—called roving—from hobby shops or specialist wool merchants. It comes in natural colors or already dyed.

Materials

Wool roving: Don't get anything other than pure wool; it will be harder to spin. Some of the lanolin should still be in the fleece if possible; this makes it easier to handle.

Drop spindle: There are many drop spindles from which to choose. I recommend looking for a rim-weighted spindle, for it will spin slower and will be easier to control as an absolute beginner. It's probably best to look for a low-whorl spindle—one that has the bulk of its weight at the bottom. A notch in the spindle to guide the wool is optional.

Cost: The spindle is going to be the most expensive item. Basic spindles range from $15 upwards. Expect to pay around $3 an ounce or more for the roving, but many places do offer discounts for higher volumes. I'd suggest more than an ounce to start with; the finer the wool is spun, the longer the strand the roving will produce.

Time spent: There is no set time for this. Spinning takes a lot of practice; it's not something that will be mastered in an hour or two.

However, persevere with it; 4 ounces of nicely spun wool will be enough to knit or crochet a lovely scarf!

Start Spinning

Well, not quite. Before the spinning can be started, it's necessary to pull out some of the fibers and twirl them with your fingers as if you were twisting them into a thin rope or thick thread, to give them the direction. This is called drafting, and it is the very essence of spinning. Keep doing this until there is a uniform thickness of yarn and around 18 inches in length. There's a skill to this; not twisted enough and the fiber will fall apart, too much twist and it won't pull out properly.

This piece is called the leader. Tie the leader onto the spindle; assuming you are using a bottom rim spindle, you will tie the knot under the rim and spiral the leader up the spindle the way that you will continue to spin—most spinners spin clockwise. Practice, practice, practice letting the weight of the spindle wind the leader around the shaft. I find it most comfortable to put the spindle in my right hand and the yarn in my left; try it both ways and see which works best for you. Keep working with this leader, winding it and unwinding it on your spindle until there's a fluid action with the spindle spinning smoothly.

Now you're ready to start spinning! It's best to do this sitting down. Twist the spindle clockwise with one hand and feed it from the leader with your left hand (or the opposite if it's more comfortable). Remember to keep the leader consistent; this is what governs the thickness of yarn. Don't expect it to be perfect, because it won't be. If you've got the action correct, the twist will run up the leader and then take more fibers from the roving. It's this repeated action that makes the spindle spin the fiber.

When you've got a length that is as long as your arm, it's time to wind it onto the shaft of the spindle. Once the action is fluid and comfortable and you're capable of spinning a short drop and allowing the spindle to land in your lap, it's time to stand up. Instead of your lap stopping the spindle, it will dangle until it stops spinning on its own. Don't let it twist backward; this is when another twist is added and the spindle spins again.

Clear as mud, isn't it? It's very hard to describe spindle spinning because each spindle behaves differently, so I've included some resources below. It takes ages to get the hang of it, but once you do, you can explore using vegetable fibers like cotton or flax. You'll also be able to drop the spindle nearly anywhere and get on with the business of creating your own yarn—and you'll no doubt be quite the conversation piece too!

Further Reading

Spinning with a Drop Spindle by Christine Thresh, 1974.

Respect the Spindle: Spin Infinite Yarns with One Amazing Tool by Abby Franquemont, 2009.

Spin It: Making Yarn from Scratch by Lee Raven, 2003.

Online Resources

Because it is often easier to do something by copying than by reading about it, I highly recommend you check out these two YouTube videos (and others) to see just what the words have instructed you to do:

"Drop Spindle for Beginners—Complete Tutorial," by JillianEve.

"How to Spin Yarn Using a Drop Spindle #1 Tutorial Spinning Series," by ElfdaughterCrafts.

Reference

"Imbolc." The Free Dictionary by Farlex. Farlex. Accessed July 29, 2020. https://www.thefreedictionary.com/Imbolg.

Candle Magic

Ember Grant

IMBOLC IS AN ANCIENT Celtic celebration believed to have been celebrated around the first or second day of February. At Imbolc, we celebrate the stirring of new life that is soon to emerge in nature. This is a sabbat believed to be associated with birth and lactation due to the lambs born at this time of year.

Spiral Spell for Growth

One of the symbols associated with birth is the spiral; it represents endurance and the continuation of the cycle of life. Spirals have been found in ancient art of many cultures including Celtic, Hindu, Aztec, Maya, and native North American nations.

One meaning ascribed to the spiral is that it represents the origin of the universe; it can also illustrate a coiled spring filled with energy. Spirals are found in nature in the shapes of shells and in the patterns of growth in seeds and petals. Many ancient peoples noticed these patterns and incorporated spirals into their art. It stands for possibility, expansion, and evolution.

In addition to spirals, plants are the perfect analogy for the Wheel of the Year. They either endure by root systems and seeds or they complete their life and return to nourish the earth—either way, they are an ideal symbol for the Wheel of the Year and for the life cycle. We, too, leave something of ourselves in a variety of ways when we depart. This is different for everyone, but we must not forget that we're part of the cycle. We will use the spiral symbol and plant imagery in this spell to stimulate regeneration and growth for whatever goal you have in mind.

You will need white candles (any number, any size, but keep them uniform and use all of one type: tea lights, votives, tapers, or pillars) and a piece of paper approximately 6 x 8 inches.

You can use this spell to simply honor the sabbat or focus on a specific goal that you wish to manifest. Write your goal on the paper. Roll the paper and flatten it into a strip. Then roll the strip the other way to make a spiral shape. Make it small enough to hold in your projective hand. Wrap your fingers around it. Project your will and energy toward the goal. Focus. Visualize your goal as a seed growing into a strong and sturdy tree. Seeds are pure potential— and so is your intention.

Place the paper on a secure surface and arrange the candles in a spiral moving outward from the paper.

Chant as you place the candles:

Resting roots and sleeping seeds
beneath the soil and snow,
waking up and reaching out—
to grow and grow and grow.

Allow all the candles to burn out. Unfold the paper, expand it, and keep it somewhere safe as you work toward your goal.

Candle Anointing Ritual:
Preparing Candles for Magical Use

A common part of spiritual and religious practice is that of anointing. Many people anoint themselves in order to prepare for ritual or ceremony—this is typically done by using oils or perfumes, water, incense, or other substances. The process of anointing something is to consecrate it, prepare it for a special experience, and put ourselves in a state of mind beyond the mundane. In magical practice, we create sacred space for ritual, and our tools should be sacred too. This includes candles. This is a practice you can use for any spell or ritual at any time of year.

Preparing a candle for ritual depends on the candle—did you make it yourself or buy it? Chances are, if you created it, then it's ready to be anointed for a specific magical use. If you purchased it, you may want to cleanse it first. The act of cleansing and clearing removes unwanted energies. The anointing process is a bit different. This act makes the candle "sacred" and ready for magical use. It's a way of designating it for a purpose—similar to the way you "charge" a crystal, for example.

To cleanse a candle, you can purify it with incense smoke, let it rest on a bed of salt, or use salt water. Misting with salt water is a quick and easy method. Simply add warm water to a clean spray bottle and dissolve a few grains of sea salt in the water. This is a great way to cleanse and clear a candle before anointing it.

A common practice for anointing or "dressing" candles is to use essential oils. It is recommended that essential oils be diluted in carrier oil since some of them can be harmful to the skin. You can also dilute essential oils in a bit of water. Once diluted, the oil mixture can be applied with your fingertip. If you prefer to use full-strength oil, apply it with a small brush that you reserve for this purpose. (And be sure to rinse the brush after each use.)

You can simply touch the oil to the candle's surface, top, or bottom, or you can "draw" a simple symbol with the oil. Some people trace a circle around the candle's surface. It's up to you. It also depends on the type of candle. These methods work well for votives or pillars, but for candles poured into containers, you can just apply the oil to the top. Use the candle immediately after anointing it. Large pillar and three-wick candles may benefit from repeated anointing if you only burn them occasionally.

There are other benefits to anointing your candles. Using essential oils can also add an extra layer of intent and effectiveness to your purpose if you choose oils based on the specific ritual or spell you're performing.

In this case, the act of anointing is the ritual itself. You can easily integrate this into your creation of sacred space, or just perform this simple ritual before a candle spell.

Here's a simple chant to use for your anointing process:

This candle is no more mundane; it's magic fire, sacred flame.

Reference

Nozedar, Adele. *The Illustrated Signs and Symbols Sourcebook.* New York: Metro Books, 2010.

Imbolc Ritual

Lupa

IMBOLC HAS A VARIETY of symbols associated with it besides sheep: fire, white and red, and the goddess Brigid. If you so choose, decorate your ritual area with these colors and symbols. You might drape your altar with red and white cloth; some may even wish to use a sheepskin. Candles, of course, are quite appropriate, though keep them away from the aforementioned sheepskin! If you wish to honor Brigid or other deities, include statues or other depictions of them.

Sheep Ritual

This ritual is centered on the spirit of Domestic Sheep, and so it's a good idea to make her presence particularly prominent. While you can certainly include nice paintings and statues of sheep, nothing says you can't also have an adorable stuffed toy lamb in attendance; just use whatever you have on hand. Some may choose to also have a sheep skull in addition to or instead of the sheepskin. Lamb or mutton is an appropriate food, especially with an evergreen herb like rosemary, and all prepared with great respect and gratitude. (You may wish to purchase the meat a few months in advance and keep it in the freezer, as it may be easier to find in the summer and fall when many sheep farmers are processing lambs.) For those of a vegetarian or vegan sort, or who don't care for mutton, a "bread lamb" is also a perfectly good substitute, and there are lamb-shaped baking tins perfect for the job.

You will also want to have warm winter clothes in the circle with you. These can be ritual-only or your everyday cold weather gear, so long as they are clean. Have a warm, sweet (but not alcoholic) drink as well, preferably in an insulated container. Hot chocolate made with real milk is a particularly good option if resources and dietary restrictions allow.

Begin the ritual indoors. Do not light the candles yet; use an artificial light instead—the dimmer, the better. Cast your circle and invoke whatever entities you prefer in whatever manner you normally do so. Call on Sheep to join you:

I invite you, Ovis aries, she who has walked beside humans for thousands of years, to join me today (or tonight). Be with me, with your rounded belly and your warm wool and your nourishing milk, and be honored in this place.

Then curl up on the floor (you can add a cushion or fluffy blanket to make it more comfortable). As you feel Sheep arrive in your ritual area, imagine that you are a tiny lamb curled up within her womb, safe and warm. If you are celebrating alone, imagine these words, or if you are in a group, have one person say the following:

Greetings and joy to you, for this is a time of new life! But be wary as well, for safety is not assured. Let us go out to greet the world and see what it offers us. As I give my lambs warm wool to keep them safe, so now shall you don your own warm layers.

Get up and put on your winter clothing and pick up your warm drink. Go outside, whether that is into your yard or to walk around your neighborhood. As you cross the threshold from the warm indoors to the chilly outdoors, imagine that you are embracing this world for the very first time. Pay attention to how the cold air feels on your skin and how, even with the warm clothing you wear, you may still feel the chill. Imagine what it must be like to be a tiny newborn lamb being born into a day or night like this, or perhaps even colder, with only its mother to protect it.

Now, take a sip of your warm drink, and as you do, imagine these words or have someone in your group say them:

Blessings, little one, and welcome to the world! Though it be harsh, there is still much good in it. Feel the warmth of my milk and the nourishment it offers. Know that even in these cold times the spark of life still burns.

Head back indoors to your ritual area. Light the candles and let that be your only light, if practical. As you warm up again, continue to sip your drink, feeling the heat from within and without chase away the chill. Imagine that you are that tiny lamb curled up against the warm side of its mother, belly full of milk, and ready for a well-earned nap. (Be careful not to actually doze off—the ritual's not quite done yet!)

Imagine or say these words:

All of life is like this, a blend of the cold and the warm, the safe and the dangerous, the joy and the sorrow. Today (or tonight) we stand on the precipice of change, and ahead we can smell the sweet flowers of spring, even as the chill of winter still nips at our heels. We ask you, Sheep, to guide us through these times, to show us that even those who are most taken for granted may yet have much strength and resilience to offer, and to let us always look at the world with clear eyes so we may truly appreciate what is there. We thank you, Sheep, for your time with us tonight, and we honor you this Imbolc!

Close the circle and see the deities and spirits off as you will, then extinguish the candles and finish that drink before it gets cold.

Notes

Notes

Notes

Notes

Ostara

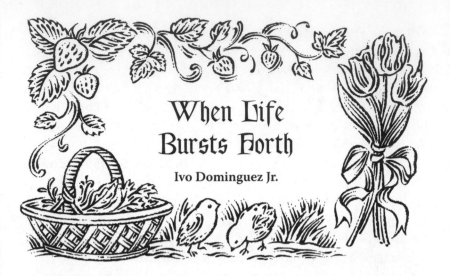

When Life
Bursts Forth

Ivo Dominguez Jr.

ALTHOUGH MANY PEOPLE FOCUS on the equal length of day and night as the defining feature for the Spring Equinox, for me it is the entry of the Sun into Aries. From the perspective of astrology, Aries is the beginning of the zodiac, of the story arc that is the journey through the year and symbolically through all cycles. Incidentally, astronomers measure the start of the earth's orbit each year at the Spring Equinox. Aries is the first and most primal fire that lit the stars, that shone on the first day, and sparked the magic called life. The Spring Equinox is the dawn and birth of the year. If you keep this in mind, you'll always find your way to the focal point for all the ideas related to this sabbat.

In the path I follow, the wheels of time, the cycles of nature, are all nested within each other. In a sense, daybreak in the diurnal cycle, the first quarter moon in the lunar cycle, and the Spring Equinox are all in the same station but at different levels. There is a similarity and resonance between each of these as if they were different hues of the same color. There is a practical use to understanding these connections as well. If you can start your celebration or rituals for the Spring Equinox near dawn, you will feel its power more clearly. If your schedule doesn't let you celebrate on the day of the Spring Equinox, you could use the first quarter moon nearest to

Ostara as an alternative date. Another possibility is to observe the Spring Equinox at dawn on the closest date that fits your schedule.

You've probably noticed that I have alternated between using the terms "Spring Equinox" and "Ostara" in this article. Ostara is the most common designation for this holiday in the Pagan community and I use it frequently, but it is also one of the names of a Germanic goddess of spring for which we have very limited recorded history and lore. However, the imagery of hares, eggs, flowers, and a goddess surrounded by an awakened earth has gained in power over the last few centuries as the fitting representation of the coming of spring. In years where my observances and rituals include the goddess Ostara or make extensive use of this symbolism, I tend to call the holiday Ostara. In years when that is not the case, it feels more respectful to not use her name, and so I default to calling it the Spring Equinox or sometimes Aries Ingress. If you are a Druid, it may be that you call this holiday Alban Eilir: Light of the Earth. There are many names for this holiday in various Pagan traditions.

Here is a chant that I wrote in 2007 that has served well in our Ostara celebrations and rituals (Assembly of the Sacred Wheel).

"Sweet Water, Warm Sun"
Sweet water and warm sun bless us
Sweet water and warm sun bless us
Oh, spring comes hope—begins in us
Oh, spring comes hope—begins in us
Out come the leaves,
Up comes the grass
Oh, seeds and eggs, oh Ostara
Oh, seeds and eggs, oh Ostara

The association of seeds and eggs with this sabbat goes deeper than the symbolism of new life. Seeds and eggs are like little universes unto themselves and are a great representation of a microcosm. I like to imagine that seeds contain a miniature world tree. I like to imagine the bright yellow yolk in an egg as a sun shining within. They both wait balanced on the edge of beginning until the conditions of the outer world, the macrocosm, trigger the cascade into life. The seed awaits the sun's warmth, the spring rains, and the touch of soil that announce that it is time to start. When a chicken lays a fertilized egg, it cools down and the spark of life within hovers and hangs waiting for more eggs to be laid each day. When there are enough eggs, the hen sits on her clutch. The eggs warm back up and the magic of life begins.

The Spring Equinox is also a time to open your senses, both physical and intuitive. It is a time for spring cleaning of the soul so that you will be affected by the beauty of the season. Also, becoming more open and more present will allow you to hear and feel the message that it is time to begin. You are a part of your world and are called to awaken and grow just like the seeds, the buds, and the eggs. It will happen whether or not you are aware of it, but if you are a conscious participant in the process, you will gain so much more.

The March Equinox is also World Storytelling Day, International Astrology Day, Mother's Day in several Middle Eastern and African nations, New Years for some Eastern nations, and many other celebrations as well throughout the globe. Anthropologist Margaret Mead advocated that Earth Day, which was founded by John McConnell, be held on the March equinox rather than the April 22 date that most people use. I encourage you to research other holidays that are on or adjacent to Ostara, especially local or regional festivals and observances. You may find some inspiration in these parallel holidays in planning your Spring Equinox festivities. For example, you could have a day of stories, songs, and poems about springtime. We've included offerings to our mothers, grandmothers, great-grandmothers, and so on at some of our Spring Equinox rituals.

Unless you live at the equator, the equinoxes are the only two days of the year when the sun truly rises in the east and sets in the west. The rest of the year, the sunrises and sunsets are offset either to the north or to the south of the cardinal points. In all the places

I've lived since I became a witch, I've made a point of identifying the windows that most closely align with the east and the west. I place flowers or seeds on their windowsills or other objects to honor the sun's journey from east to west on the equinoxes. If you have a garden or an outdoor ritual space, the Spring Equinox is an excellent time to place stones, posts, or other durable markers in the east and west as determined by the sun's position. Using a square, you can infer north and south. These cardinal points will be true rather than the magnetic directions given by a compass, which deviate from true depending upon your location.

Day and night are of equal duration at the equinox because the sun's path across the sky equally honors the light and the dark in its steady course from east to west. It is about more than just day and night; the equinox is about balancing any and all qualities that seem to be opposites, antonyms, complementary, or contrasted with each other. During the two equinoxes, the tilt of the earth's axis is perpendicular to the sun's rays. This means that at noon at the equator during the equinoxes, the sun is directly overhead. Magically and symbolically, this means that the force of the sun reaches to the core of the earth. The whole earth shares in this illumination equally.

The Spring Equinox is about the birth of new life and the growth and reinvigoration of all that is perennial. Think about how these qualities and energies work separately and in tandem as you dream up their best uses for your purposes. Initiations and self-dedications are special kinds of new beginnings, and the Spring Equinox favors and blesses these and similar actions. Healing work, meditation, or practices that bring about greater self-integration also benefit from the harmonizing properties of the Spring Equinox.

Coming into balance and maintaining balance is a dynamic process that requires both effort and finesse. When the Wheel of the Year turns to the Spring Equinox, the power of poise builds so that the runner can explode into action, the diver can leap from the board in their flight to the water, and the bud can swell and unfurl. The current that flows through this holiday can be used to remove obstacles, to break a stalemate, to make a long-postponed decision, to open new roads, or liberate you from the chill of a wintry heart. Although many people tend to focus more on the devotional or the celebratory aspects of the eight sabbats, they are also a time for magic applied to purposes.

In your quest to learn more about Ostara, the Spring Equinox, you are likely to find lore and customs that describe cultures, plants, animals, landscapes, and weather conditions that may be quite different than the ones you experience. Some may suggest to you that it is better to ignore all that and focus on what is present in your locale. Others may suggest, especially if you are a part of a formal group, that it is better to look to the roots of the traditions. Either approach can be made to work well, but you can also find a middle way between the two.

Ask yourself what parts of the lore that you uncovered in your research were particularly compelling and stirred you? Look to see if there is a plant, an animal, a custom, and so on that is local to you but has a similarity of energy and meaning. Then test your hunch by adapting it and adding it to your celebration. It may need to be refined for the coming year or it may need to be tossed out so something else can be tested. Think about the qualitative changes that occur in your life and the lives of your community in the spring. Is there a story, a song, a poem, a recipe for a feast, a seasonal decoration, or so on that needs to be created to express the nature of spring where you live? Let intuition, trial and error, and fresh insights guide you to creating a local and authentic way to work the sabbats.

The glyph, the symbol for Aries (♈) contains some of the mysteries of this sabbat. The first thing that comes to mind is that the glyph is a simple representation of a ram's horns. It is a fitting emblem for the animal will to live, to move, and to push away whatever blocks its path. It is the red force of life, the instinctive drive to survive, to thrive, and become abundant. If you look again, the glyph can be interpreted as the two leaves of a seedling breaching the surface of the soil. It is the green force of life that adapts, that is tenacious, and enriches the earth. This glyph also symbolizes a third thing that requires a closer look with a quiet mind. The Aries energy is also the light, the fire, at the beginning of things both in linear time and in eternity. The glyph can be seen as the one becoming the many as spirit enters into the physical realm. It is the radiant force of spirit, a geyser of light, a vortex of possibilities, the enduring, endless life that does not fade. The ritual for the Spring Equinox included at the end of the Ostara section uses the threefold pattern of the green, red, and silver flames of Aries as its basis.

Ostara, the Spring Equinox, the Aries Ingress, or whatever name you may use for this sabbat, brings hope and the reassurance that life always triumphs. This sabbat also shows us the pragmatism and wisdom of nature in the wild exuberance of growth and fertility during this season. Not all the flowers will produce seeds, not all those seeds will sprout and grow to maturity, but enough will. Spring will always provide a new beginning, one that is the same yet different than all that came before and will come again. Blessings of the spring upon you and yours.

Reference
Assembly of the Sacred Wheel. "Sweet Water, Warm Sun." March 23, 2015. YouTube video, 2:03. https://www.youtube.com /watch?v=U60MnCH3yIQ.

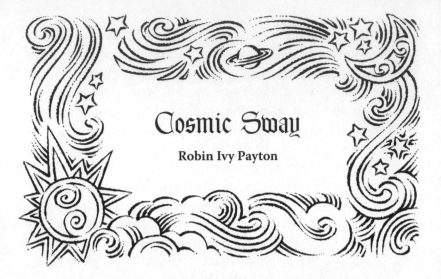

Cosmic Sway

Robin Ivy Payton

OSTARA ARRIVES WITH THE vernal equinox when light and darkness are equal. The balance of night and daylight happens twice each year, now as we welcome spring and again when autumn returns. Daylight Saving Time starts on March 13 in the areas that honor the time change; the ground basks in sunshine, and warmer days begin. The Sun travels over the celestial equator, moving north in the Northern Hemisphere on Sunday, March 20, 2022, at 11:32 a.m. EDT, the time of the vernal equinox. Soon, seeds are planted, leaves bud on the trees, and we witness regeneration both externally and internally as our yearning for spring is fulfilled.

Astrology for Ostara

Ostara follows the Full Moon of March 18. Full Moon in Virgo relates to health and routine. The Pisces Sun highlights emotions and sensitivities. With added influence from Neptune and Pluto, deep feelings are due for release and resolution. Trust your intuition, especially in matters of physical and mental wellness. Stay away from foods or other products you may be sensitive to. Finish creative projects and add artistic style to everyday tasks. People may need extra care and compassion now. Do everything with love.

The Sun moves to Aries as the equinox arrives. Aries is a call to action and development. Venus, Mars, and Saturn tour forward-thinking Aquarius, encouraging experimentation, innovation, and turning visions into realities. On this day of balance, the Moon first graces Libra, the sign of polarities such as yin and yang, female and male, dark and light. Pluto squares the Moon, bringing intimacy issues to the surface. This leads partners, in either love or business, to face conflicts or questions while seeking equitable and honest answers. The Moon is void of course from 8:40 a.m. to 11:44 a.m. EDT, when the Moon then moves to Scorpio. Use these hours to create sacred space, meditate or journal, and ease into the seasonal change. This is a magical Moon sign for the rites of spring.

New Month, New Moon

April begins with a New Moon at 2:24 a.m. EDT. The Moon and Sun ring in the first full lunar cycle of spring. Mercury, the planet of thoughts and communication, is close to Sun and Moon, stimulating new ideas, plans, and actions. Aries New Moon leads us to experiment or start over. Notice what really inspires feelings of motivation and inner fire. The next two days raise innovative, air sign energy, as the Moon connects with Venus, Mars, and Saturn in Aquarius. Aries provides the initiative and Aquarius offers collective and technological support. This is a positive time to initiate a conversation, relationship, or project to settle a disagreement and make a fresh start. Upgrade systems and devices that connect people, assist in communication, and foster community development.

All planets are in direct motion during this New Moon. Look for clear paths where obstacles have finally, or suddenly, been removed. While the Sun, Moon, and four planets tour fire and air signs, act with the energy of the phoenix, a symbol of vitality and regeneration. Time your announcements, changes, and advancements close to and after New Moon arrives, avoiding void of course times. On April 2, avoid the hours from 9:51 a.m. to 12:50 p.m. EDT. There is also one long void Moon from 11:15 p.m. to 11:30 a.m. EDT between April 6 and 7. Check for other void of course times, which are shorter or further away from New Moon. Actions are best taken outside of those hours when important points or details may be skimmed over, forgotten, or lost.

Jupiter and Neptune in Pisces

As the equinox and New Moon pass, Jupiter approaches Neptune in Pisces, where the two meet on April 11. Traits associated with both planets are amplified, leading to growth and emotional healing. Pisces qualities of faith, generosity, and compassion are also enhanced. As with everything, there are shadow sides as well. Within arising opportunities, be also aware of any duplicity. In personal affairs, keep trust in balance with skepticism. Satisfy your curiosities and ask for clear terms and information. Let wisdom override any tendency toward denial. Ultimately, this conjunction can lead to spiritual transformation for oneself and for humanity.

The Rabbit and the Robin

Animal spirits for Ostara include the rabbit and the robin. Both reflect the sign Aries in different ways. As Aries is the zodiac's first sign, the rabbit is a symbol of new life. Both the sign and the animal are known for the ability to move quickly and to leap. Rather than steady movement, the rabbit hops forward. Astrologically, rapid developments and actions are expected this spring. Rabbits are adept at both freeze and flight, and when in danger can move between those states readily. They instinctively know when and how to take a different turn. Tune in to Rabbit energy to stay out of harm's way while knowing when it's beneficial to change course.

Robins share Aries's astrological color, red. Often seen as a sign of spring, robins sport rosy chest feathers and respond to this color. Male robins even communicate about territory through their red breasts. Akin to Aries's competitive nature, these birds will physically confront each other or affirm their territory through loud and boastful songs. As a spirit of spring, Robin says sing your own tune; like Aries, Robin paves their own way. Symbolically, Robin relates to new growth and creative force, the essences of Aries and spring.

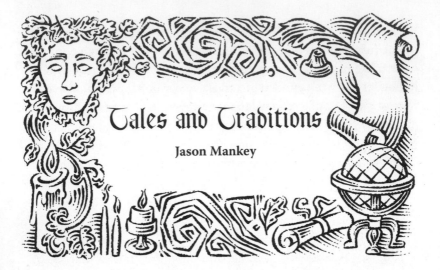

Tales and Traditions

Jason Mankey

IF YOU GREW UP in a Pagan or Christian household, it's likely that you've hunted for either plastic or hard-boiled eggs in the springtime. My favorite Easter memories as a child had nothing to do with church and everything to do with those egg hunts! Today as a Witch, I host Ostara egg hunts for my coven and find just as much delight in the whole enterprise as I did as a child. Whether we play games with them, hide them, use them in story and ritual, or simply dye them, eggs are an inescapable part of early spring!

Ostara: The Incredible Magickal Egg

The egg is the perfect symbol of spring because it encapsulates exactly what's going on around us. The darkness of winter is finally overtaken by the lengthening days, and as the sun grows in power in the sky, new life emerges from the ground. Even in places where winter's grasp remains firm, spring's potential can be felt stirring at Ostara. Eggs are justifiably praised as symbols of new life and fertility but, perhaps even more than that, eggs are symbols of potential. Eggs can hold new life or, perhaps, just breakfast.

Our ancient ancestors revered eggs, and every continent on earth (with the exception of Antarctica) has at least one culture with a creation story involving an egg. This creation egg is often called "the world egg" and generally emerges out of chaos or some sort of primordial sea. Sometimes the entire universe is born inside this egg, and in other versions of this type of myth, the egg cracks, with the top of the egg becoming the sky and the bottom the earth. The Orphics of ancient Greece believed that the world egg emerged out of various primordial forces such as time and fate, which in turn birthed the hermaphroditic god Phanes, who then created the other gods and much of the universe.

Eggs make sense as a symbol of the awakening earth in the spring, but no one is quite sure when the tradition of sharing colored eggs in March and April began. However, there is a direct link between pagan Rome and colored eggs, and it comes to us from the second century Roman emperor Marcus Aurelius (121–180 CE). According to legend, on the day of Aurelius's birth, April 25, his mother's hen laid eggs speckled with red. The eggs were taken as a sign that baby Marcus would grow up to be a great emperor. When Aurelius eventually assumed the throne, eggs dyed red began to be passed out around the empire in his honor (Newall 1971, 265 , 268).

In many parts of Europe, especially in Eastern Orthodox areas, Easter eggs are still traditionally red. Though there are Christian legends surrounding the custom, it's more likely that red eggs began as a Pagan way of celebrating Marcus Aurelius, or perhaps the dyed red eggs come from an even older custom that's been lost to history?

For centuries eggs have been an important source of protein, and in many cultures, eggs were often the only easily available means of protein. During the Middle Ages, eggs were often given as gifts to priests and other religious figures as a form of payment on major holidays (Hutton 1996, 198). Often, these eggs were handed out in baskets, a possible origin for the inescapable "Easter basket" that's so common in March and April. During the Christian season of Lent (the six-week period preceding Easter) the eating of eggs was banned in many European countries, leading children to decorate the eggs they were not allowed to eat.

Eggs have been used for divination for thousands of years and are still used for this purpose in many parts of Europe and the Americas. To divine the future with an egg, the shell of the egg was generally pierced with a needle or other sharp object, and the white, which dripped from the egg, was collected in a glass of water. The images that appeared in the water were then interpreted to tell the future. (Some countries preferred interpreting the yolk rather than the egg whites, so if you choose to do this, either way is fine!) A much messier version of egg divination comes from France where eggs were once smashed on a person's head. The resulting mess was then interpreted by the person who broke the egg (Newall 1971, 334).

Eggs can also be used for good luck and to remove negative energies. During the early modern period, it was customary to leave eggs as an offering to evil spirits and malicious Witches. Once the spirit or Witch accepted the egg as a gift, it was believed they would never return (Newall 1971, 69). Deformed or yolk-less eggs were thought to carry bad luck, and in parts of England such eggs were tossed over houses to send the bad luck away (Newall 1971, 71).

Today, images of Witches on broomsticks are hard to escape, but in many parts of the world (including France, Germany, Mexico, and Russia) Witches also rode broken eggshells to their sabbat meetings. In addition to riding on eggshells, it was believed in many places that Witches also used eggshells as cups and plates when celebrating a sabbat (Newall 1971, 80–81). Because of these strange ideas about Witches and eggshells, it was customary in much of Europe to make sure an eggshell was smashed into very small pieces after being cracked (Newall 1971, 83). (What's never explained is how Witches use something as small as an eggshell to get around; simply cracked or broken up into tiny pieces, eggs aren't that big!)

People have been playing games with eggs for hundreds of years, and it's possible that some of these games have origins in paganisms past. Games involving eggs in Northern Europe might have arisen from simple celebrations honoring the return of spring and being able to get out of the house. Egg rolling, which is most associated today with the front yard of the White House, is centuries old and might have originally been a charm meant to fertilize or awaken the earth. Even if that wasn't the game's original intent, it's an interpretation that makes sense at Ostara and can easily be adopted by Witches. Whatever you do to celebrate spring this year, be sure to include an egg!

References

Forbes, Bruce David. *America's Favorite Holidays: Candid Histories*. Oakland, CA: University of California Press, 2015.

Newall, Venetia. *An Egg at Easter: A Folklore Study*. With a foreword by Robert Wildhaber. Bloomington IN: Indiana University Press, 1971.

Feasts and Treats

Elizabeth Barrette

Ostara is the first of the spring holidays. It speaks to the promise of the season just as it begins to unfold. Featured symbols evoke fertility, fecundity, and abundance. It is the first burst of exuberance after winter loses its icy grip on the world.

Greek Lamb Chops

Lamb is a traditional spring food across many traditions. Fertile herds make this meat readily available during the season. Lamb is hearty, yet more delicate than beef. It matches wonderfully with feta, a crumbly cheese made from sheep milk.

    Prep time: 15 minutes, plus 4 hours
    Cooking time: 5 minutes
    Servings: 4

2 lemons (zest and juice, about ¼ cup)
¼ cup full-flavor extra-virgin olive oil
½ teaspoon sea salt
½ teaspoon black pepper
¼ teaspoon dill seeds
1 bay leaf
4 lamb chops

2 tablespoons light olive oil
2 teaspoons dried sweet marjoram
2 teaspoons dried sweet basil
½ cup crumbled feta cheese

Wash two lemons. Zest them into a large zip bag. Cut them in half and juice them into the zip bag.

Slowly drizzle in ¼ cup of full-flavor extra-virgin olive oil, whisking to combine it with the lemon juice.

Add ½ teaspoon sea salt, ½ teaspoon black pepper, ¼ teaspoon dill seeds, and 1 bay leaf. Whisk again to mix everything together.

Close the bag and allow the marinade to sit at room temperature for 10 minutes.

Put 4 lamb chops into the zip bag and close it. Allow the lamb chops to marinate in the refrigerator for four hours.

Put 2 tablespoons of light olive oil into a skillet and turn it on high.

Remove the lamb chops from the bag. Discard the bag and remaining marinade. Coat the lamb chops thoroughly with dried sweet marjoram and dried sweet basil, until both sides look fluffy and green.

When the olive oil is hot enough to shimmer, put the lamb chops in the skillet. Cook for 2 minutes. Flip the lamb chops over and cook for 3 minutes.

Serve the lamb chops alongside crumbled feta cheese. This recipe makes 4 servings.

Herbed Mushrooms

Mushrooms grow best in cool, damp conditions. Wild ones burst into glory during spring, and cultivated ones are plentiful in stores. Cheese makes the recipe richer. Herbs add complexity of flavor, and a topping of fresh parsley gives a bright green touch.

Prep time: 10 minutes
Cooking time: 15 minutes
Servings: 4–6

cooking spray
16 ounces baby bella mushrooms
1 clove garlic, minced
1 teaspoon dried oregano
½ teaspoon dried thyme
¼ teaspoon rubbed sage
¼ teaspoon dried crushed rosemary
½ teaspoon sea salt
¼ cup full-flavor extra-virgin olive oil
4 ounces shredded metsovone or provolone cheese
½ cup fresh Italian parsley, snipped

Preheat the oven to 400°F. Spray a 9 x 9-inch casserole dish with cooking spray.

Rinse the mushrooms to remove any remaining compost, holding them gills-down so they don't get soggy. If the stem ends are woody, trim them off. Remove any bad spots. Compare the size of the mushrooms. If some are much bigger than others, cut the bigger ones in halves or quarters so that all the pieces are approximately the same size. Gather the mushroom pieces in a large bowl.

Peel 1 clove of garlic. Mince it and put it into a small bowl.

To the bowl add 1 teaspoon dried oregano, ½ teaspoon dried thyme, ¼ teaspoon rubbed sage, ¼ teaspoon dried crushed rosemary, and ½ teaspoon sea salt. Pour in ¼ cup full-flavor extra-virgin olive oil and stir to combine.

Put the mushrooms in a large skillet and turn the heat on medium. Pour the herb mixture over the mushrooms and stir to coat them evenly. Cook the mushrooms at medium heat, stirring so they don't burn, until they soften and release their juices. This typically takes about 10 minutes.

Use a slotted spoon to scoop the mushrooms out of the skillet and put them in the casserole dish. Cover the top of the mushrooms with shredded metsovone or provolone cheese, about 4 ounces.

Bake the mushrooms at 400°F until the cheese melts, approximately 5 minutes.

Remove the casserole dish from the oven. Use kitchen scissors to snip about ½ cup fresh Italian parsley over the top of the mushrooms.

Baked Asparagus

Asparagus is among the earliest vegetables ready for harvest. It is most affordable in spring. Herbs also leaf out early. Lemon basil adds a bright note to the spice and symbolizes the returning sun.

Prep time: 5 minutes
Cooking time: 10–15 minutes
Servings: 3–4

1 bunch of asparagus
2 tablespoons full-flavor extra-virgin olive oil
1 tablespoon lemon juice
½ teaspoon thyme
¼ teaspoon dried dill weed
¼ teaspoon dill seeds
¼ teaspoon sea salt
¼ cup lemon basil, chiffonade

Preheat the oven to 400°F. Line a baking sheet with aluminum foil.

Rinse 1 bunch of asparagus. Grasp each stalk by the ends and bend it until the bottom end snaps off. (The bottoms can be saved for use in stew or stock.) Pat dry the top spears and set them aside.

Into a large zip bag, put 2 tablespoons full-flavor extra-virgin olive oil, 1 tablespoon lemon juice, ½ teaspoon thyme, ¼ teaspoon dill weed, ¼ teaspoon dill seeds, and ¼ teaspoon sea salt. Shake gently to combine the ingredients.

Add the asparagus spears to the bag and zip it closed. Gently squeeze and tilt the bag to coat the asparagus spears with oil and herbs.

Spread the asparagus spears on the baking sheet, distributing them in a single layer so they don't touch. If there is olive oil left in the bag, drizzle it over the top of them.

Bake the asparagus spears at 400°F until the stalks are tender and the tips turn crispy, about 10–15 minutes. Check toward the end to make sure they don't burn, as some ovens have hot spots.

To chiffonade lemon basil: Pick off the large leaves. Stack them together. Roll the leaves into a cylinder. Use kitchen scissors or a sharp knife to cut across the cylinder, making narrow ribbons. Continue cutting until you have about ¼ cup of lemon basil chiffonade.

Take the asparagus spears out of the oven. Transfer them to an oval serving platter, arranging them in a neat parallel pile like a stack of logs. Place the lemon basil chiffonade over the middle of the asparagus spears.

Crafty Crafts

Charlie Rainbow Wolf

IN THE NORTHERN HEMISPHERE, we're well into spring by the time Ostara comes knocking. The shops are full of images of Mother Earth awakening, from baby chicks to spring flowers. It's a time when eggs are represented in chocolates and jelly beans, and of course, egg dye!

There are many theories as to why we dye eggs. When I was growing up in Indiana, my Sunday school teacher taught us eggs were first dyed red to symbolize the blood of the crucified Christ. My English husband says he remembers learning something about King Edward I coloring eggs to give as gifts. Colored eggs seem to have played a role in many cultures throughout history.

Dyeing Fabric

It's easy enough to make the jump from dyeing eggs to dyeing fabric. It's possible to use commercial dyes but much more fun to scavenge natural items and see what colors they produce. If you spun wool at Imbolc, you might even want to dye that for Ostara!

Materials

Fabric: This needs to be a natural fabric like wool or cotton, otherwise the dye might not take. If you are new to dyeing, I recommend a white, 100 percent cotton fabric. Consider sackcloth tea towels; they take the dye well, they're fairly inexpensive, and they're easily available online or in stores.

Mordant: This is a fixative for the dye and influences the final hue of the color. Common mordants are alum, iron, tannin, and even table salt.

Dyestuffs: I'm focusing on what can be gathered naturally rather than store-bought colors. Onion skins and rhubarb leaves are among my favorites. Experiment with this and have some fun; I've made suggestions below.

Dyebath: This is a big stockpot for the mordant and dye. An iron pot will add its own mordant. It's a good idea not to use the same pot for food preparation.

Cheesecloth or other strainer: Nut milk bags are suitable and easy to use—and reuse. They're available from farm stores, home canning suppliers, and online retailers.

Rubber gloves: You don't want to dye your hands!

Distilled water (optional): Regular tap water will do unless you want to be very precise about the final color. The chemicals in tap water might influence the outcome.

Candy thermometer (optional): This will come in handy for measuring the temperature of the dyebath.

Cost: Again, this is hard to estimate, as an absolute fortune could be spent on a new stockpot and fabrics and mordants, or you could scavenge what you have and do this at little or no cost. If items are purchased, consider looking for 100% cotton sheets or even white cotton shirts from a local charity shop. Sometimes old stew pots or stockpots can be found there too. A new stockpot could cost $30 or more. Sackcloth towels average less than $3 each (cheaper if a bundle is purchased), and simple mordants such as alum or salt are in the region of $10 or less a pound. The nut milk bags are $5 or so—if one isn't available, use an old nylon stocking! If a candy thermometer is desired, they can be obtained for under $10. Work within your budget; there are few hard and fast rules.

Time spent: One hour to mordant the fabric and another hour to dye it. These do not have to be consecutive.

The Mordant

The dye process is quite simple and consists of two parts: mordanting the fabric and dyeing it. Mordanting the fabric can be done quite quickly—when I lived on the farm, I used the hot cycle of my old twin tub washing machine. The general rule of thumb is to use 100 g of mordant to 500 g of fabric—a 20 percent ratio.

Fill the dye pot ½–⅔ full of water. Dissolve the mordant into the water and gradually heat it to hand hot—somewhere near 120°F if a thermometer is used. Slowly immerse the fabric, and let it steep in the hot liquid for 45 minutes, keeping the heat constant. Give it the occasional gentle stir. The mordant bath can be reused for several different pieces.

Remove the material from the mordant and allow it to cool. Keep it damp; if it isn't going to be dyed immediately, put it in a ziplock freezer bag and store it in the refrigerator or other cool container. It should keep for 5–7 days.

The Dyebath

This is the exciting bit, where you get to add the colors. I've listed some of the items I've used when dyeing cotton and the colors they produce. They're common household items, and if one isn't available, then choose another—be daring and experiment!

Yellow: celery leaves, rhubarb leaves, Queen Anne's lace roots
Orange: carrots, onion skins
Green: mint leaves, grass, nettles
Blue: elderberries, red cabbage
Purple: pokeweed, basil leaves
Brown: dandelion roots, walnut hulls, tea, coffee

There's no hard and fast rule to the amount of dyestuffs to use per dyebath. The higher the quantity of dyestuffs, the deeper the color of the dye. Use whatever is around; it might be helpful to keep a record of what works and what doesn't for future reference.

Bring the dyestuffs to a slow boil then let them simmer for at least half an hour. When the dye is a good color, carefully strain it. An alternative to this is to tie the dye materials into cheesecloth or a straining bag or even an old nylon stocking before boiling, but I find more color is released if the straining is done afterward.

Once the strained dye is back in the pot, heat it to just simmering (around 185°F) and slowly add the material to be dyed. Keep it simmering gently for 30–45 minutes, stirring it occasionally to help it color evenly. Turn off the heat and let it cool naturally in the dye, again stirring occasionally.

When the dyebath is cool, put on the rubber gloves and remove the material from the liquid. The dye can be reused a few times, but it is likely to give paler results each time. I've seen spinners do this so their wool knits up in an ombre. Rinse to remove any excess dye, and when the water runs clear, hang the material up to dry.

Dyeing is as complicated or easy as you make it. Another fun way of dyeing is to put the mordanted fabric and the dyestuffs in a large canning jar and set it in the hot sun for several days. This is a fun activity to do with the kids—and it teaches patience!

Further Reading

Harvesting Color: How to Find Plants and Make Natural Dyes by Rebecca Burgess, 2011.

Passion for Color by Sarah Burnett, 1990. (This was my go-to book for ages.)

Vegetable Dyeing: 151 Color Recipes for Dyeing Yarns and Fabrics With Natural Materials by Alma Lesch, 1970.

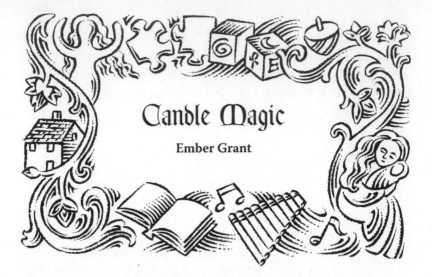

Candle Magic

Ember Grant

Spring, as the time of rebirth, is the perfect time for floating candle spells. Why? Because these candle spells also utilize the element of water—a powerful symbol of cleansing, renewal, and birth. The creation myths of many cultures begin with water.

Displays of floating candles are enchanting to the eye and can be truly powerful as magic—they're an ideal way to combine all four elements into a spell. The candle represents both fire and air, then you have water to float the candle on, and you can add earth by the type of container you use or by putting crystals or herbs and flowers in the water.

Floating Candle Spells

Floating candles are available in a variety of colors and shapes, but small plain white or ivory ones (approximately the size of tea lights) are inexpensive and relatively easy to find. The type of candle you use is your choice—as long as it floats.

Glass bowls or containers work best because they keep the water visible and allow you to see decorative items such as stones or plant materials. You can use just about any shape or size, as long as it accommodates the number of candles you need.

Fire-Infused Water

This spell is intended to create infused water that you can use for other magical purposes after the candles burn out. This standard recipe is intended for basic renewal, but it can be adapted for a variety of purposes, as you'll see.

You will need:

Container for water (your choice of size and shape)
White floating candles (one or more, your choice)
Clear quartz cluster or point
One small grain of sea salt

Put the salt and crystal into the container, then add the water and candle. This water can be used to anoint magical tools or other objects (or yourself). It can also be added to a refreshing magical bath. Light the candle and visualize the power of the fire element infusing the element of water, and the water mingling with the energy of the crystal.

Adaptations

For each of these, add ingredients to the standard recipe as indicated; the plant materials can be fresh or dried. Choose one or more stones from the list or use all of them. Put stones into the container first and add water followed by plant materials before adding the candle.

Cleansing and purification (to remove negativity): three small sprigs of rosemary, three drops each of frankincense oil and cedar oil, one cluster of lavender flowers (or one drop of oil), citrine, kyanite, Herkimer diamond, or black tourmaline

Protection: one leaf each of basil and holly, one rose thorn, a piece of oak bark, three pine needles, six drops of rosemary oil, pyrite, tiger's-eye, iron, or garnet

Prosperity and success: a pinch of ground ginger, five peppermint leaves or three drops of peppermint oil, a sassafras or oak leaf or piece of oak bark, one drop of patchouli oil, tiger's-eye, or malachite

Love: a daisy flower or cluster of lavender flowers, five rose petals, one cluster of yarrow flowers or one violet, a sprig of rosemary, emerald or rose quartz

Psychic ability (dot on third eye): a pinch of ground cinnamon, one cluster of yarrow flowers, five drops of lemongrass oil, lapis lazuli, moonstone, amethyst, or sapphire

You can adapt the standard recipe to suit your specific need. There are endless combinations of herbs, oils, crystals, shells, and candle colors.

After the candle burns out, strain any plant materials and bury them; save the water in a tightly sealed container and use within a year. Cleanse the crystal and dispose of the candle wax as you choose. If desired, you can keep the crystal in the container with the water.

"Fire in Water" Spell for Inspiration and Wisdom

Water was very important to the Celts. There is evidence they believed water was magically potent—it was the source of wisdom and inspiration in addition to holding the power to heal and transform. They viewed special bodies of water as emerging from a sacred source in the otherworld—a great well of wisdom. And they're not the only culture whose mythology reveals a reverence for water. But there's something noteworthy about the fire and water combination that we can connect with.

According to *Celtic Cosmology and the Otherworld* by Sharon Paice MacLeod, their cultural cosmology contained a concept of "fire in water," the spark of creative power, a "fire" was said to reside in some special bodies of water; a special "wisdom and … manifestation of poetic or prophetic skill" (MacLeod 2018, loc 4819).

Use this spell to evoke that divine wisdom and creativity. Visualize yourself being open to receiving boosted mental power and stimulation. You'll need a floating candle, a glass container or bowl, and any combination of herbs, oils, and stones from this list:

Herbs: your choice of seven rosemary leaves or a sprig of spearmint (fresh or dried)
Essential oils: honeysuckle, lilac, rosemary (combine as desired)
Stones: ametrine, celestite, jade, kunzite, kyanite, Picasso stone, sodalite, tiger's-eye, turquoise, yellow fluorite, or clear quartz

Visualize your intent as you put water in the container, add your chosen ingredients, and place the candle on the water. You can place the arrangement on your desk or other creative workspace. As you light the candle, chant and visualize your specific goal or need.
Chant:

Fire in water, bring wisdom—inspire.
Fire in water, bring power—burn higher.

You don't need to let the candle completely burn out—you can snuff it and relight it as desired to invite the spark of inspiration. After the candle burns out, discard it as you choose. If you wish, you can use the water to anoint your creative tools; otherwise, pour it out in a safe place along with the plant materials.

Reference
MacLeod, Sharon Paice. *Celtic Cosmology and the Otherworld.* Jefferson, NC: McFarland & Co., Inc. Kindle edition, 2018.

Ostara Ritual

Ivo Dominguez Jr.

THE CHIEF ENERGY THAT is offered by the Spring Equinox is the fire of life ascendant. This ritual summons this fire in three of its forms. First, it is called as the green flame of the plant realm, of the green life, and will bring us the power to grow and flourish. Second, it is called as the red flame of the animal realm, the red-blooded ones, and will empower us to seek and find what we desire. Lastly, it is called as the silver flame of the spirits, the bright ones, and will show us wisdom and understanding.

Rite of the Green, Red, and Silver Flames

This ritual may be enacted solo or as a group ritual with minor changes, and is easily adapted to match your path and style. Ideally, the ritual should be performed the day of the Spring Equinox, and if that isn't possible, then on the full moon before or after it. It may be done indoors, but it benefits from being done under the dome of the sky.

Preparations

You will need three white jar candles, one for each of the flames. Measure and cut three pieces of paper that can be wrapped around the candles to half of their height. Decorate each strip of paper so that one represents the flame of plants, one the flame of animals, and one the flame of spirits. Depending upon your preferences and artistry, these embellishments could be simple drawings, collages, keywords, sigils, or simply colors. If you are doing this ritual with others, this can be a group effort. You can use a bit of clear tape to attach these to their respective candle. In a pinch, you could use three tea candles in mason jars. What matters here is that you put your energy into making these devotional candles.

Place the three candles on a small table in the center of the space you will be performing the ritual in. Visual cues often improve the experience of a ritual so consider using a tablecloth with a color or pattern that represents spring. Arrange the candles so that they form a triangle and place a leaf or seed next to the green flame candle, an egg or bone next to the red flame candle, and a crystal or pentacle next to the silver flame candle. It is easier if you light the candles before beginning the ritual. As you light each candle, envision the flame becoming the color needed for this working: one green, one red, and one silver. Take a deep breath and push some energy into each candle until it feels right.

The Ritual

The rite begins with purification, but think of it as a spring cleaning for the senses—both physical and subtle—rather than the standard of cleansing with incense and salt water. You could ring a bell or tap on a drum and revel in the purity of the sound. You could gaze upon the rich colors of a bouquet of spring flowers and then breathe in their fragrance. You could brush your fingertips over a seashell or embroidered fabric to take in its shape. You could put a grain of salt or a drop of honey on your tongue and focus on the flavor and the sensation. These are suggestions, and you can dream up other options so long as you activate at least three of your senses. Then proceed with your normal method for creating sacred space, if you have one, including invocations for any deities or spirits that are a part of your practice.

Go to the central altar, pick up the green flame candle, and walk outward in a growing spiral while repeating:

By leaf and flower and fruit
I call the green flame forth

When you feel the power of the green world, the realm of plant life buzzing and thrumming around you, spiral inward and return the candle to its place on the altar. As you repeat these words and the subsequent calls in this ritual, speak with rhythm and power, and allow your intonation and pitch to change as it will.

Go to the central altar, pick up the red flame candle, and walk outward in a growing spiral while repeating:

By breath and blood and bone
I call the red flame forth

When you feel the power of the red world, the realm of animal life, its heartbeat and its dance around you, spiral inward and return the candle to its place on the altar.

Go to the central altar, pick up the silver flame candle, and walk outward in a growing spiral while repeating:

By above and below and life eternal
I call the silver flame forth

When you feel the power of the spirit world, the realm of ethereal life, its silver bells and the tingle of cool electricity, spiral inward and return the candle to its place on the altar.

Now stand facing the altar (if it is a group, link hands if possible) and say:

The power of spring surrounds me, is in me, and moves through me!
The power of spring surrounds me, is in me, and moves through me!
The power of spring surrounds me, is in me, and moves through me!

If you are doing this ritual with a group, drop hands. Close your eyes and pause to concentrate on what you are feeling, thinking, and sensing. When you are ready, open your eyes and use your own words to ask the flames for the growth, the drive, the wisdom, etc. that you need at this time. If you are uncertain about what you need, then ask for guidance to find your way forward. When you (or all) are done, then chant:

Fire, fire, soul's desire
Changer change me
Burning, burning, higher

You may also listen to the chant to learn the melody (Assembly of the Sacred Wheel). It is better if you sing, as more power will be raised, but you can just repeat the words in a strong voice.

As you chant, move your gaze from candle flame to candle flame to draw their power into yourself. Continue to chant and give yourself enough time to take in as much power as you can hold. Once you reach your limit, approach the altar and pass your hand over each candle so you can feel the heat. You may free-form tone or "aum" at this point to bring the energy to a peak and end the chant. Place your hand over your heart and feel the truth of the changes that you have requested, and speak your preferred magical closure declaration, such as "blessed be," "so mote it be," "it is done," etc. Then offer words of thanks for what you have received. If it is a group working, after the last person has been to the altar, it is time to close the ritual.

To end the ritual, extinguish the candles in the order of green, red, and silver. If it is your custom to snuff candles, do so, but there is another option in this ritual. Lift up each candle, one at a time, and blow the candle out while visualizing its light spreading outward to infinity. While doing this, set the intention that the flame will carry your requests for change to all the places and beings that will assist you. Next, if you included your own method for creating sacred space at the beginning of the ritual, use your standard closing. This concludes the ritual, but it would be good to write down notes to document your experience and review the outcomes at the Autumn Equinox.

Reference

Assembly of the Sacred Wheel. "Fire Soul's Desire." March 23, 2015. YouTube video, 1:50. https://www.youtube.com /watch?v=9ToICvsCzoc.

Notes

Notes

Notes

Notes

Beltane

Beltane Fragaria
Suzanne Ress

BELTANE, OPPOSITE TO SAMHAIN in the Wheel of the Year, is a major fire festival celebrated traditionally from the eve of April 30 through May 1. Great magical restorative bonfires meant to cleanse, purify, and render fertile the earth, domestic animals, and humans alike were lit as evening fell.

Beltane is also a solar festival celebrating fertility, birth, motherhood, and the blossoming forth of all new life. In ancient times, Beltane was when the Great Mother got together with the sun god (sometimes known as the Green Man) and, following their lead, human couples also united sexually, perhaps playfully in the shadows beyond the bonfire or in the woods after the traditional maypole dance.

It is believed that the earth's reproductive and sexual energies are at their peak at Beltane, and with Beltane, the light half of the year begins. Beltane Eve is a likely time for fairies to be seen, and one of the preferred foods of fairies is the wild strawberry (*Fragaria vesca*), which is abundant from mid-April to mid-June, and especially sweet and luscious at Beltane.

Bees, bumblebees, and butterflies pollinate the little white flowers of wild strawberry plants when there isn't too much else in bloom to satisfy their pollen and nectar needs. When these small, ripe red heart-shaped berries come, with their lovely sweet scent and juicy flavor, they are a perfect representative fruit for Beltane.

It is not only fairies who love wild strawberries; hedgehogs do too! Yes, hedgehogs will gorge on them, and so will field mice, foxes and their kits, and many other wild mammals and birds. Whether cooled by night dew or warmed in the midday sun, these little morsels are beloved by many, including humans. Wild strawberries have been eaten by humans since at least the middle Paleolithic era (Lemmers).

In case you are not familiar with wild strawberries, they are a lot smaller than cultivated strawberries—about as big as red currants—but with a much sweeter, intense strawberry flavor. These are not to be confused with false wild strawberries, or Indian mock strawberries (*Potentilla* or *Duchesnea indica*), which produce yellow rather than white flowers and a tasteless non-poisonous red fruit easily confused by non-experts with real wild strawberries. The real ones are unmistakable because when you walk near them you will smell a strongly luscious, sweet strawberry perfume.

Wild strawberries grow by above ground runners and rhizomes, and, given the right soil, light, and moisture conditions, will spread rapidly to cover large areas of ground.

For hundreds of thousands of years, wild strawberries were prized as a spring treat by humans and were foraged by people all over Europe and the Americas until, around the Middle Ages, monks and other people with gardens started transplanting them into their herb and kitchen gardens. The wild strawberry's qualities remained the same until the 1700s in France when the first cultivar was created. That was the *Fragaria x ananassa*, the same one most people are accustomed to finding nowadays in the supermarket, often year-round. The cultivated strawberry is much larger, smells great, and is juicy, but is generally not nearly as sweet and flavorful as the wild strawberry.

From the original cultivated strawberry came hundreds more cultivated varieties: small ones, large ones, late-producing, early-producing, long-producing, deep ruby red, white, yellow, purple, you name it. One well-known special strawberry cultivar is the Little Scarlet (an offshoot of *Fragaria virginiana*, which was originally the North American wild strawberry). It was brought to Essex, England, from North America by the Wilkin family in the early 1900s and is grown only at the Wilkin family's Tiptree Estate to be made into preserves by Wilkin & Sons.

Another notable cultivar is the pineberry strawberry. This is a white strawberry with red seeds and a pineapple-like taste. White strawberries are considered to be alright for people with a strawberry allergy to eat. White Alpines, another white strawberry good for allergy sufferers, are small, like wild strawberries, but, of course, white.

Strawberry Mythology

Some Native American Indian tribes have long associated wild strawberries with spring and rebirth, as they are the first wild fruits to ripen. They used them mixed with cornmeal to make strawberry bread, which white settlers then transformed to strawberry shortcake, a traditional Memorial Day weekend dessert.

During medieval times, the strawberry signified perfection and righteousness and strawberry fruits also symbolized esteem, love, purity, passion, health, and perfection, and were a popular embroidery motif. In heraldry, depictions of strawberry leaves were sometimes used to denote rank.

Strawberries are one of Venus's symbols, due to their red heart shape. Frigga, the Norse marriage goddess, was believed to smuggle dead children to heaven by hiding them in strawberry patches. Both Freya, the Norse goddess of love, and the Christian Virgin Mary have been associated with strawberries.

Dutch early surrealist artist Hieronymus Bosch painted one of his most famous works, the triptych *The Garden of Earthly Delights*, in the fifteenth century. It is now housed at the Museo del Prado in Madrid, Spain, and, if you are unfamiliar with Bosch's work, it is wonderfully strange. The center panel, which represents a lustful earthly paradise, features many oversized strawberries. At the bottom right are two human-sized strawberries, one bursting open to emit round blue balls, and the other being used as an exercise ball by a naked woman. Further up on the right side of the same panel is a forest glade scene depicting a group of naked men surrounding one seated naked woman. One of the men is offering the woman a strawberry as big as a melon. Another giant strawberry, with fairy wings, rides on the back of a naked man, a spiny tail emerging from a slit on its side.

About thirteen years ago, my husband and I purchased our small farm. At the time, it was not yet a farm but merely a partially built abandoned house on a large parcel of hilly agricultural land. In May, when we first came to look at it, the "lawn" around the shell of the house consisted of overgrown wormwood, plantain, stinging nettles, dandelions, and many other greens and grasses. There was one low-growing large swathe, a carpet of wild strawberries, in front of the house, which, when we walked across it, gave off such a strong, sweet perfume that it seemed we had entered a jam factory.

We made regular visits through the month of May to pick containers full of these wild strawberries while we waited for the building permits to be granted.

When, finally, we'd gotten the permits, contracted a construction company, and had the work of finishing the house done, a couple of years had passed. Because of all the heavy trucks driving over the "lawn," the wonderful strawberry carpet was nothing but a field of mud.

Later, a landscaping crew arrived, plowed the dirt, planted a traditional lawn, and put up a sprinkler system. For a few years, we had a fairly normal grass lawn, but, little by little, wild plants, greens, and grasses blew in and self-sowed. Not so secretly, I was pleased to see the lawn becoming wild again and purposely mowed around the patches of daisies, mother-of-thyme, Mary's eyes, and whatever else I liked. A couple of years ago, while mowing, I noticed a small patch of wild strawberries where once there was the carpet, and I allowed it to stay. Each time I mowed the lawn, I observed with satisfaction that the patch was spreading, becoming once again a magic *Fragaria* carpet.

Our neighbor's toddler daughter, whose favorite fruit is strawberry, loves to sit down in the center of this *Fragaria* carpet during the Beltane month, searching for and picking the little whole strawberries to eat when she comes to visit. Of course, when she gets up, the seat of her pants is stained with spots of strawberry juice.

She gave me an idea, and one May evening I threw caution to the wind and lay myself down on the magic *Fragaria* carpet after dinner (and a couple glasses of wine). Fireflies twinkled all around me, and I could see the waxing half moon through the tree leaves above me. I closed my eyes and breathed in the sweet fragrance deeply, feeling the cool of the strawberry leaves, listening to the last of the croaking frogs. It seemed the perfect setup for a fairy visit and, in fact, it wasn't long before I fell into a half-sleep state. It seemed that the *Fragaria* carpet was lifting off the ground and hovering a foot or two above the yard, taking me with it for a magic carpet ride. Through half-closed eyes, I saw many glowing little spirits zipping about all around me on the carpet. Were they fireflies or were they fairies? Something extraordinary was going on. I lay there, amongst the fairies, being carried about, out of the yard, away from familiar territory, into a Bosch-like surreal world of lusty pleasure for a length of time I could not measure and, when I finally arose, I felt unusually revitalized, my clothes stained and perfumed with strawberry juice.

The Fairies

At Beltane, you are perhaps more likely than at any other time of the year to see, or otherwise sense, the presence of fairies. A twilit walk along a quiet woods path, a meditation in a flower garden, or just relaxing on your porch as the sun goes down and the moon rises are all good ways to increase your chance of witnessing a fairy visit.

Traditionally, some food and drink from the Beltane festival was offered to the wee folk.

In parts of Bavaria, it was traditional come springtime to tie little bags or baskets of wild strawberries to the cows' horns to appease the fairies and elves, and to protect the cows.

Some of the fairies' preferred gathering places at Beltane are "fairy rings"—circles of wild mushrooms; as well as circles of lawn daisies, patches of wild violets, patches of wild thyme, and, most of all, swathes of wild strawberries. It is here that groups of fairies gather to celebrate Beltane and gorge on their favorite fruit. If you would prefer that they play no tricks upon you over the course of the year, you may wish to leave them a dish of freshly whipped cream to accompany their strawberries on the eve of April 30. And if you are lucky enough to catch a glimpse of them, do not speak or move suddenly, and especially do not try to take a picture of them, as these actions startle and tend to anger them, and they will likely take revenge on you through trickery. Just stay put and, rather than gawking, close your eyes halfway—this will make them easier to see.

Once our house was mostly finished and we'd moved in, I invited several people over for a Beltane celebration on the evening of April 30.

I had created a hidden glade in the woods at the top of the hill with wooden benches, flowers and flowering bushes, an in-ground firepit, a few found garden statues, and a mosaiced chair I'd made over the winter, depicting the young buck I'd seen in those woods numerous times. I'd placed a circle of slate stepping-stones around the fire pit and planted myrtle and ivy all around it. This became a special, magical, sanctified place, and it was where our coven started to hold its celebrations and rituals.

For Beltane, I had invited a few people from outside of our coven, and among these was a male friend who had expressed interest in a female friend of mine he'd met several times at parties, so I invited her too. She arrived with an unexpected surprise—a Tupperware container of fresh strawberries and another one of whipped cream.

We went through our ritual by the light of garden torches, a little fire in the pit, and candle lanterns and, when we'd finished, it was time for cakes and ale. The group broke into smaller units and people ate and drank and conversed and had fun. I had lost sight of my male friend and the strawberry woman, but when I did see them again, she was hand-feeding him strawberries and whipped cream, and each time she gave him a finger full of whipped cream, he sucked and licked it off sensually. It wasn't long before the two of them disappeared together somewhere, out of the visibility afforded by the flickering firelight and, shortly thereafter, they initiated a long and loving relationship. Had the Beltane fairies had something do with it? My guess is yes!

Reference

Lemmers, Nadine. "Food in the Stone Age." Hunebed Nieuwscafe. September 2016. https://www.hunebednieuwscafe.nl/2017/01/food-in-the-stone-age/.

Cosmic Sway

Robin Ivy Payton

THE WHEEL OF THE Year turns to Beltane on the weekend of April 30 and May 1, 2022. The Sun has come of age with strong light and heat, on the way to Summer Solstice. As the Earth receives the Sun, they cocreate as goddess and god. Seeds planted after spring equinox sprout and bloom as the trees green and blossom. Traditionally, celebrations begin on the last night of April, the eve of Beltane. During the week that follows, the Sun reaches the cross-quarter point, midway from spring to summer on Friday, May 6. It's a special year as Beltane stretches between weekends and syncs with the Taurus New Moon.

Astrology for Beltane

On April 30, the eve of Beltane, the Sun and Moon unite in harmony with Mars at 4:28 p.m. EDT. Time spells and rituals close to this Taurus New Moon. The earth element of Taurus is feminine and receptive. The natural world thrives with observable, tangible examples of creation and rejuvenation. Use all your senses to draw upon these energies to fuel your intentions. Love, sexuality, devotion, and emotional stability are themes of this lunar cycle. Prosperity and other forms of abundance are also favored by Taurus, a sign of comforts and acquisitions. Most planets are in direct motions for forward momentum, for moving toward goals, and allowing life to naturally unfold. Note that this lunar cycle is known for long-lasting effects. Make promises you plan to keep and agreements you can abide by. It may be challenging to reverse what begins during Taurus New Moon.

Beltane fire rituals and parties are well timed as sensual Taurus Moon extends into the morning of May 2. Open the five senses to colors, scents, and sounds of springtime. Notice textures, touch the earth, and embrace the one you love. Beltane is a feast of the lovers, the goddess and god, the bees and the flowers, sexuality and coming of age.

Emotional peaks are likely as four planets in Pisces connect with Taurus Moon. The dynamic quality of Mars, expansiveness of Jupiter, and dreamlike feeling of Neptune flow through New Moon and Beltane. Loving Venus in Pisces, planet of beauty and the divine feminine, forms the final aspect before the Moon moves void of course May 2 near daybreak. This brings sweet morning vibes and feelings of pleasure. During the short void of course transition, from 6:13 to 6:46 a.m. EDT, linger in the sentiments of the weekend before beginning your Monday routine.

As an earth sign, Taurus strongly correlates with the physical self, and with the arrival of Beltane, your body's needs may change. As the season progresses and the weather warms, consume foods or supplements to address seasonal allergies or any feelings of fullness or excess. Banish post-winter sluggishness by rising with the sun, brushing your skin before bathing, and adding neck stretches and heart openers to your daily routine. Stimulate warmth, particularly if you live in a northern or cooler climate. In general, the human body responds to more vigorous and frequent exercise, lighter cooked foods like steamed vegetables and legumes, fruit juices, and local honey at this time of year. Focus on internal wisdom by observing your body's responses to food, drink, and somatic movement, and support yourself through the social and environmental shifts that come with middle spring.

The Cross-Quarter Day

Friday, May 6, 2022, is the cross-quarter date, when the Sun is midway between vernal equinox and Litha, the Summer Solstice. Some may choose this date for celebrations of Beltane. The waxing Moon in Cancer is in harmony with Uranus, the Sun, and Mars. Moods and plans may be changeable as the Moon and Uranus align. For this reason, outline alternative or backup plans in case of last-minute shifts.

Family activities are favored under Cancer Moon. Imagination, creativity, and physicality blend as the Moon and Mars tour water signs while the Sun is in earthy Taurus. Play at shapeshifting with children's games or yoga poses like cobra and cat. Free the mind and let the body take over through performance, dancing, and role playing. As weather permits, partake in summertime enjoyments, such as bare feet in grass and cool water.

The waxing Moon in a fertile sign lends itself to gardening and planting. Beltane is a time for encouraging growth through nourishment and care. Astrologically, this cross-quarter day is also suitable for cleaning, repairs, improvements, food preparation, and a bit of indulgence. The Cancer-Taurus dynamic shines for house parties and reunions. Gather with loved ones for celebrations of May as Mother's Day weekend begins.

Astrological Symbols

Images of the Empress and Mother Earth resonate with Beltane. In the tarot, she is the third card of the major arcana, often pictured in a lush landscape with a baby in her belly and a crown upon her head. The fertility of the Empress signifies gestation of any kind, from childbearing to long-term projects such as writing a book or building a home. At Beltane, the Sun is her mate, contributing to fertilization and progress. Number 19 in the major arcana, the Sun depicts a happy child, suggesting joy and youth. These and cards of the pentacles suit align with Taurus season. Include them in spells or display them as reminders of what you intend to grow. Infuse your intentions with pink and green crystals or candles to align with Taurus energies including formation, fruitfulness, and procreation. Rose quartz opens to love and relationship, while jade offers the nurturing influence valued by this sign. Wear precious green emerald for contentment and bliss. In the garden, invite bees, hummingbirds, and other pollinators by tending to flowering plants. Invoke these creatures in meditations and journeys as they teach the healing powers of flowers and how to draw in the nectar of life.

Festival of the Sun

The Summer Solstice returns on June 21, 2022, at 5:14 a.m. EDT in the Northern Hemisphere. On this festival celebrating the powers of both goddess and god, the Sun offers the year's longest stretch of daylight. Solstice comes from the Latin word *solstitium*, which translates as "Sun stands still," and from sunrise to sundown, when the weather is clear, we immerse in light. Yet, even on a cloudy or rain-soaked solstice, the Sun is there with energetic power that penetrates the clouds. A day like this, if it happens, reminds us that the Sun and other heavenly bodies have just as much influence when obscured from our earthly view.

From a scientific perspective, the Sun appears at maximum elevation at noontime on this day and for a few June days on either side. The Solstice moment comes when the Earth's axis points directly toward the Sun and the tilt of the earth toward the Sun peaks. Our ancestors built monuments and structures to track the cycle of the Sun and the passage of time. They knew the Sun as their source of heat and light, essential for survival. In present time, we may find more spiritual than practical meaning in structures such as

Stonehenge in England or Chichen Itza, the Mayan pyramid. With modern technology, humans no longer rely on sky watching for agricultural purposes or telling time, yet our need for and love for the Sun is constant. Litha marks a time to celebrate in the warmth and abundance of solar energy.

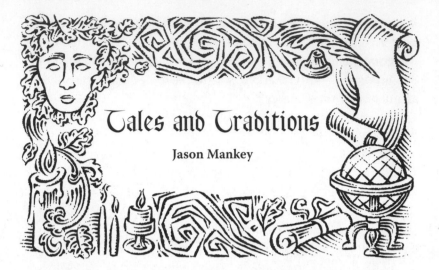

Tales and Traditions

Jason Mankey

WHEN MOST WITCHES THINK of Beltane, they tend to conjure up images of flowers and maypoles in their mind's eye. A smaller percentage might think of events traditionally associated with the German Walpurgis and picture Witches flying on brooms to celebrate under a full moon. What most Witches don't think of is fire, and yet fire might be the oldest Beltane tradition of all.

The Fires of Beltane

The first written reference to Beltane (spelled "Belltaine" in the text) dates from the year 900 CE and comes from *The Sanus Chormaic* (also known as *Cormac's Glossary*), an Irish glossary attributed to Cormac mac Cuilennáin, an Irish King and Christian Bishop. In Cormac's entry on Beltane, he states that the word Beltane means "lucky fire" and that the holiday was presided over by Druids. He also writes that the purpose of the holiday was to safeguard cattle, and that livestock were run between two fires to protect them from disease (Cormac 1868, 19).

By the year 900 CE, Ireland had been Christianized for several hundred years, so Cormac's description of Beltane does not come from firsthand information. It's likely that Druids presided over at least some Beltane celebrations amongst the Irish-Celts, but by the year 900, "Druid" was often used as a general term for a diviner or a user of magick, and because there were far more cattle than Druids during the days of the Irish-Celts, it's likely that a wide-ranging group of people probably oversaw Beltane activities (Hutton 2009, 38–39). Anyone who was proficient with magick could have led the cattle through the Beltane fires.

Activities similar to the ones described by Cormac (minus the Druids) were a part of Irish celebrations of May Day well into the nineteenth century. There were slight variations of course, cattle may have been encouraged to jump over a (small) fire instead of running between two of them. But such activities share enough in common to suggest that there was most certainly a common origin point, an ancient Pagan holiday celebrated near the first of May.

For many modern Witches, Beltane is a purely celebratory sabbat. With winter completely over and the heat of high summer still a few months away, the start of May is generally a very pleasant time (and it would have been the same in ancient Ireland). However, for people who relied on the cattle they raised for sustenance, there were always things to worry about it. Disease was a constant threat, but there were less mundane concerns as well.

Even today, many people in Ireland and other parts of the world worry about the Fae (fairy folk) and the havoc they might unleash on livestock. The Fae were thought to sour the milk of cows who belonged to humans they did not like and were capable of far worse if circumstances warranted it. Fear of the Fae was very real, and the tricks they played on humans were taken very seriously.

Farmers in nineteenth-century Scotland were especially scared of Witches rather than fairies! It was believed that on the night of May 2 large bands of Witches roamed across the Scottish countryside casting spells to sour the milk of cows and promote disease and other maladies amongst the livestock. According to folklorist Walter Gregor in his 1881 work *Folklore of the North-East of Scotland,* farmers kindled large fires on the night of May 2 that they called *bone-fires* to keep evil Witches away from cattle and corn (Gregor 1881, 167).

Despite the name "bone-fires," the protective fires generally used substances like hay and straw for kindling. Instead of running their cattle over or between the bone-fires, the evening's fires were taken out among the livestock and grain crops on poles or pitchforks held high overhead. Those without a pitchfork or pole stayed near the fire and danced around it shouting: "Fire! blaze and burn the witches; fire! fire! burn the witches" (Hutton 1996, 222). If you have any neighbors today who engage in this activity, it's probably best if you don't invite them over for Beltane.

Gregor also writes that in certain areas large cakes of oat or barley were rolled through the ashes. After the cake and everything else in the fire had been burned up, the ashes were taken from the bone-fire and then scattered around the farm for protection. The scattering of the ashes was not done in silence either, Gregor says those doing the scattering did more screaming at the local witches, crying "Fire! burn the witches" (Hutton 1996, 219).

In the Scottish Highlands, farmers petitioned the Beltane fires directly to keep their livestock free from disease, malicious magick, and certain predatory animals. On the night of May 1, farmers would gather around a large fire and cook a simple meal. Once the meal was finished cooking, they would pour some of it onto the ground as a libation. From there, they would each divide up an oatcake into several smaller pieces and petition the fire to spare their cows, sheep, and horses. Tossing the small pieces of cake over their shoulders and into the fire they would say, "This I give to thee, preserve thou my horses," or whatever other animals they were worried about (Pennant 1776, 111).

Once petitions had been made to the fire, the farmers would repeat the ceremony, but this time invoking the names of certain predatory creatures to leave their livestock and draft animals alone. Author Thomas Pennant in his *A Tour in Scotland 1769* writes that the farmers would say things like "This I give to thee, O Fox! Spare thou my lambs." He also recounts other animals the farmers were worried about such as crows and eagles. The night ended with celebratory drinking and the meal that had been cooked earlier. The remains of the dinner and the fire were then hidden by two of the rite's participants (Pennant 1776, 111).

In addition to using fire for protective purposes, there is also some curious lore surrounding home fires near Beltane. It was considered bad luck to let anyone take the fire from one's hearth on the evening of April 30 through May 1. Those that stole fire from their neighbors over that period of time were believed to gain control over those neighbors. Since it was considered bad form to steal fire from someone on Beltane, those that did so were often labeled Witches (Hutton 1996, 220). Of course, we know that Witches have much better things to do on Beltane, whether that's dancing around a maypole or sprinkling some ashes from a fire around our homes for protection.

References

Cormac. *Cormac's Glossary.* Translated by John O'Donovan. Edited by Whitley Stokes. Calcutta: Irish Archaeological and Celtic Society, 1868.

Gregor, Walter. *Notes on the Folk-lore of the North-East of Scotland.* London: Elliot Stock, 1881.

Hutton, Ronald. *Blood and Mistletoe: The History of the Druids in Britain.* New Haven, CT: Yale University Press, 2009.

———. *The Stations of the Sun: A History of the Ritual Year in Britain.* Oxford: Oxford University Press, 1996.

Pennant, Thomas. *A Tour in Scotland 1769.* 4th ed. London: Benjamin White Publisher, 1776.

Feasts and Treats
Elizabeth Barrette

BELTANE IS A HOLIDAY of love, romance, and passion. It comes at the height of spring when everything is bursting into new life. As the weather warms, outdoor activities become appealing again. Lovers take long walks and picnics in the park. Single people mingle and sometimes form new relationships. Everything is full of excitement and hope.

Flower Salad

Lettuces, herbs, and other greens are among the early harvest of spring. Edible flowers add color and a festive touch. Fresh fruit represents the sweetness of life.

Prep time: 5–10 minutes
Servings: 4–6

1 package (10 ounces) spring mix salad greens
½ cup fresh basil leaves
½ cup mixed fresh herb leaves
1 cup assorted edible flower petals
1 cucumber, sliced
¼ cup sunflower seeds
1 pint fresh raspberries, rinsed

Into a large salad bowl, put 1 package spring mix salad greens. Over the bowl, use kitchen scissors to snip ½ cup fresh basil leaves and ½ cup mixed fresh herb leaves. Toss gently.

Add 1 cup assorted edible flower petals. (I start with marigolds because they give many petals per head. Bee balm, apple blossoms, nasturtiums, pinks, roses, and violas all work.) Toss gently.

Add 1 sliced cucumber, ¼ cup sunflower seeds, and 1 pint rinsed fresh raspberries. Toss gently.

Serve with a light vinaigrette, such as the citrus one described in the Winter Solstice Salad.

Passion Fruit Smoothie

Passion fruit embodies positive energy. It encourages passions of the flesh and of the spirit. The passion vine enjoys a thriving symbiosis with ants, feeding them nectar in exchange for their protection from pests and herbivores. That makes it a great support for healthy relationships. Its extravagant flowers bloom in shades of purple, pink, and red, making them a dramatic symbol of amorous interest. In addition to the previous associations, passion fruit also relates to friendship, harmony, magic, and sleep.

Prep time: 10–15 minutes

Servings: 3

1 cup passionfruit juice

1 cup vanilla yogurt

1 passion fruit

½ banana

1 mandarin orange

2 tablespoons fresh pineapple or canned crushed pineapple

2 tablespoons fresh or frozen mango chunks

2 tablespoons fresh or frozen papaya chunks

2 tablespoons fresh or frozen strawberries

1 teaspoon freeze-dried goji berry powder or 1 tablespoon dried goji berries

1 tablespoon hemp seed hearts

1 tablespoon coconut milk

½ cup ice

(For a dairy-free version, substitute nondairy yogurt or plant milk.)

Put the liquid ingredients into the blender first: 1 cup passion fruit juice and 1 cup vanilla yogurt.

Rinse and pat dry the passion fruit. Using a serrated knife to get through the rind, carefully cut it in half. Scoop the juice and seeds out of the rind into the blender. Don't scrape hard because the rind is bitter and you don't want any of it to get into your smoothie.

Peel the banana. Cut it in half. (Save one half for the next recipe.) Cut one half into chunks and put them in the blender.

Peel the mandarin orange. Pull apart the segments to check for seeds, removing any that you find. Add the segments to the blender.

To clean a pineapple: Twist off the spiky top. Slice off the top and bottom so the fruit stands on end securely. Slice down the sides to remove the outer rind, leaving a cylinder of fruit. Cut the cylinder in half, then in quarters, then in eighths. Lay each eighth on its side and cut away the pointed edge to remove the tough core. Cut the remaining fruit into bite-sized chunks. If you don't have a fresh pineapple, you can use canned crushed pineapple, but include both the fruit pulp and its juice. Add 2 tablespoons pineapple to the blender.

To clean a mango: Slice the plump side "cheeks" away from the big seed. Use a knife to score vertical and horizontal lines through the fruit, forming cubes, without cutting through the peel. Push the peel so the cubes stick out, then shave the fruit away from the peel with a knife. Alternatively, you can use frozen mango chunks. Add 2 tablespoons mango to the blender.

To clean a papaya: Cut the fruit in half. Scoop out the seeds. Rinse the fruit. Then scoop out the soft pulp with a spoon or melon baller. You could also use frozen papaya chunks. Add 2 tablespoons papaya to the blender.

Fresh strawberries should be rinsed and patted dry. Use a paring knife or strawberry huller to remove the stem and the core around it. Drop the strawberries into the blender whole. You can also use frozen strawberries. Add 2 tablespoons strawberries to the blender.

Add 1 teaspoon freeze-dried goji berry powder or 1 tablespoon dried goji berries to the blender. Add 1 tablespoon hemp seed hearts if you want to blend them in. (If you prefer them as a crunchy topping, put 2 teaspoons into the blender now, and reserve 1 teaspoon to put on top of the smoothie when served.) Add 1 tablespoon coconut milk and ½ cup ice.

Put the top on the blender and lock it down. If your blender has a "smoothie" setting, use that. Otherwise, blend until smooth.

Chia Pudding with Tropical Fruit

Tropical fruit symbolizes the joy and freedom of the warm season. Chia seeds and plant milks create the rich base to the pudding. The spicy, floral flavor of cardamom evokes a festive mood.

Prep time: 10 minutes
Cooling time: refrigerate 4 hours or overnight
Servings: 4 (1 cup) or 8 (½ cup)

1 can (13.5 ounces) full-fat coconut milk
4 cups almond milk (18.5 ounces)
1 teaspoon vanilla extract
¼ cup sugar (if using unsweetened milks)
1 teaspoon ground cardamom
a pinch of sea salt
1 cup chia seeds
1 cup crushed pineapple
¼ cup coconut chunks or flakes
½ banana

In a large mixing bowl, combine 1 can full-fat coconut milk and enough almond milk to make 4 cups. Whisk in 1 teaspoon vanilla extract.

If using unsweetened milks, add ¼ cup sugar. Whisk in 1 teaspoon ground cardamom and a pinch of sea salt.

Whisk in 1 cup chia seeds. Wait 1 minute, then whisk again. Wait 2 minutes, then whisk again. Wait 5 minutes, then whisk again. This minimizes the tendency of the chia seeds to float to the top and form a skin.

There are two ways to serve chia pudding: One is to measure individual servings into dessert cups. Another is to put all of it into a large bowl or dessert ring. Transfer the chia pudding into your chosen container(s) and place it in the refrigerator for at least 4 hours or overnight.

Just before serving: Distribute 1 cup crushed pineapple evenly over the surface of the chia pudding. Make small piles using ¼ cup coconut chunks or flakes. Thinly slice ½ banana and make a little fan of banana slices beside the coconut on each serving of chia pudding.

This recipe makes four 1-cup servings as a light lunch or eight ½-cup servings as a dessert.

Crafty Crafts

Charlie Rainbow Wolf

FOR ME, BELTANE IS one of the most intriguing markers on the Wheel of the Year, falling opposite Samhain and between the Spring Equinox and the Summer Solstice. It's a fire festival, and fire is said to purge and purify. Among the many traditional activities associated with Beltane is that of passing through fire. You don't have to enter into the flames; build two bonfires and walk between them. In the English village where I lived, this was a traditional—but long-forgotten—event; the villagers and their livestock would pass between the fires for cleansing and blessing. I've even heard Beltane referred to as "the time of the blessing." A fire walk can be done at a group or an individual level, with the fires either raging bonfires or two simple candles. It's all down to the intent; fire is always fire.

Simple Stepping Stones

When planning a firewalk, contemplate adding stepping stones to walk on as you pass through the flames. Making your own stones from concrete is inexpensive and fun. It's necessary to plan ahead in order to give the mix time to cure, but the actual making of the stones is not time consuming.

Materials

Concrete mix: Quikrete is the brand name that I use, but any other quick-drying, all-in-one cement mix will work. If you are already familiar with pouring concrete, use the gravel, sand, and cement mix that you have on hand in a ratio of 1:2:1. Quikrete is available in 50, 60, and 80 pound bags. Don't let this deter you; we've found one 60-pound bag yields around 8 good-sized stones, and it will keep for a few months as long as it does not get damp. There's also a crack-resistant formula, which is a bit more spendy, but also worth the investment.

A mold: We use the purpose-made plastic molds available through home improvement stores or garden centers because we pour a lot and these molds can be used over and over again, so we find them well worth the money. If you are just wanting to try this to see how you like it, any plastic container will work, such as an old bucket or tub. Just make sure the bottom is flat, or you'll have a wobbly stone (which might be quite fun for a party game, but perhaps not safe around fire).

Mold release: Again, there are commercial mold releases available for purchase, but we've always used the cheap cooking spray. Any clear oil works; you don't want the concrete to stick to your mold form.

Something in which to mix the concrete: If you're planning on making many stones and mixing the whole bag of cement mix, you might want to use a wheelbarrow, as this is a good height for your back and it is easy to work the mix. My brother is a concrete mason and he uses an old piece of board on the ground and a shovel for mixing. For smaller batches, a large bucket or tub will suffice. I use an old 5-gallon shallow tub meant for serving chilled bottles of pop, picked up at an end-of-summer sale a few years ago.

Something with which to mix the concrete: I use an old garden trowel and a thick paint stirring stick.

Something with which to measure your materials: I use an empty
  coffee can.

Water

Old newspaper

Cost: Expect to pay around $3–8 for the concrete mix. If you
want to buy a mold, they range from $5 at hobby and craft shops to
$50 and more for the fancier designs from mold specialists. Mold
release is more expensive than cooking spray, which is $3–5 from
the grocery store. My mixing tub was $2 on clearance; a wheel-
barrow can top $80, and scrap board and a shovel might not cost
anything.

Time spent: This is another activity where patience is the main
ingredient. It will take you an hour or less to mix the concrete and

fill the molds. After about 4 days to a week, the molds can be removed, but it will not be ready to stand on for at least another fortnight. In this case, the longer the better.

Concrete Steps

Make sure all materials are handy. Start by spreading out the newspaper at the work area. Wash the chosen mold to remove any residue, and when it is dry, give it a light but thorough coating of the spray. This stops the concrete from sticking to the mold, so it can be reused.

Carefully measure the dry ingredients into the mixing container. Stir these together first, then slowly add water. The amount of water varies from mix to mix; the finished slop should be about the consistency of oatmeal. When the trowel is dragged through it, the sides should stand on their own but not be overly dry.

Fill the mold with the cement mix. If a bucket is used, you can determine the thickness; the deeper you fill the bucket, the thicker—and heavier—the finished piece will be. If using a purpose-made mold, fill to about ¼ of an inch from the top. Try to avoid overfilling as this has the potential to make an untidy edge on the finished stepping stone.

Place the filled mold on a level surface to rest undisturbed for at least 3 days. Resist poking it to see if it's set; this is where patience comes in! When we're in "mold making season," we tend to leave these for at least 5 days. On day 6, we remove the molds and wash them, and on day 7, we pour again.

The stepping stone is not ready to use yet! It has to cure. Place it out of the way for at least 2 weeks, giving the concrete a chance to set firm. Then you'll be ready to use it for your fire walk—and many other places, too, should you choose!

The firewalk is not the only use for making stones. We have made all sorts of stepping stones and have them throughout our herbs and around our trees as decoration, footing, and a weed barrier. Some of my friends have made their own labyrinths to walk in meditation. Stepping stones are easy to make, inexpensive, and a way of sharing with your outdoor space—or even your altar, should you not have access to a yard or garden—your own creative energy.

Further Reading

Creative Concrete Ornaments for the Garden: Making Pots, Planters, Birdbaths, Sculpture & More by Sherri Warner Hunter, 2005.

Concrete Crafts: Making Modern Accessories for the Home and Garden by Alan Wycheck, 2011.

Candle Magic

Ember Grant

At Beltane we celebrate the fertility of the land—the lush trees and flowers, the abundance of new life. Scholars are not in complete agreement about the origin of the name—some say it's associated with Belenos, a sun god. Others say the word "bel" means "brilliant" or that the name comes from "bel tene," which means "lucky fire" (Freeman 2000, 135).

Garden Blessing

The month of May is a wonderful time to perform a garden blessing. You can do it at planting time or just after planting. If it's still too early in your region for planting, save this spell for later in the season or use it to bless seeds or seedlings before planting them outside. You can also use it for an indoor garden—houseplants need blessing too!

Ideally for this spell you need a tall container or lantern for your candle—you'll be carrying it around outside and you don't want it to be blown out during the spell. But be careful not to burn yourself! The tops of some lanterns can get hot.

Since the spell requires you to allow the candle to burn out, you may wish to use a tea light since they only burn for a few hours. Or, if you prefer to use a larger candle, repeat the spell on successive days or nights, allowing the candle to burn for an hour or two each time until it's spent. You could begin during the waxing moon and complete the spell on the full moon. Alternately, perform this spell on Beltane.

If you don't have an outdoor garden, this spell can easily be adapted for any situation. If you have a balcony garden or even just a windowsill you can walk around containers or gesture around them.

If possible, perform this spell during a waxing or full moon phase. Prepare your candle by anointing it as desired, and place it inside the container.

Walk around the garden clockwise three times. The first time, chant these words and keep repeating if you have a large garden space:

Earth, air, fire, and water nourish,
help these plants grow strong and flourish.

The second time as you walk, say these words followed by the name of every plant in the garden.

By the power of this flame, I bless you as I call your name: (list the plants).

The third time, chant these words. Again, repeat the chant as many times as necessary:

Bless this garden safe and sound—
bless these plants, bless this ground.

After the third walk around the garden is complete, place the lantern or candleholder in a safe area either in the garden or near it and allow the candle to burn out. Say these words as you place the candle:

By this candle's power, bless every leaf and bud and flower.

Don't leave the candle unattended; be sure to stay nearby so you can keep an eye on it.

Optional: carry a clear quartz crystal point or cluster (or other stone of your choice) with you as you walk, and place it in the garden during your third walk around it.

Tree of Life Candle Spell

At Beltane, we celebrate the fertile earth—flowers are blooming and trees are green again (in most places). Trees are sacred in the myths of many different cultures—the idea of a world tree or tree of life is a popular symbol. In Norse mythology, the cosmos is viewed as a giant tree connecting the nine worlds that encompass all of existence. Druids are believed to have worshipped in oak groves.

The tree of life motif integrates the underworld, humanity, and the sky—a flow of energy through all levels. The motif of a cosmic tree is found throughout the world, from Europe to Africa, Australia, and China. In *The Origin of Species*, Charles Darwin uses the analogy of a "tree of life" to describe the process of evolution and the succession of species. The tree seems to be part of our human-nature connection in a variety of ways.

If you observe a tree and consider it carefully, they truly are amazing plants. Think of how long-lived some of them are—and there is such variety! And the fact they grow so big from something so small is remarkable, really. Use this spell to invoke the strength and power of trees—their longevity and stability.

Use a fairly large candle—a pillar or three-wick works best. Draw the tree of life on the candle with a branch, twig, or wooden skewer. Don't worry about how it looks; it only matters what the symbol means to you. Just draw a simple tree branching upward, then draw roots reaching down. Curve the roots up and the branches down so they connect, making a circle around the trunk. This represents the connection of all life, nourishment, and sustainability. After you finish drawing, say, "As above, so below" and anoint the candle as desired.

Surround the candle with leaves and branches from trees—ones that have fallen on the ground are fine. You can also include nuts,

pine cones, and more. If you wish, you can put the candle in a flow-
erpot or other container filled with dirt, potting soil, or mulch, and
arrange the leaves and branches around the container.

> *Root and trunk, branch and leaves,*
> *flower and fruit—sway with the breeze…*
> *grant to me…*
> *the strength and wisdom of the tree,*
> *grounded yet still reaching high,*
> *a link between the earth and sky.*

This spell can be performed day or night, on Beltane or during
any season—ideally during the waxing or full moon.

Allow the candle to burn out. You can snuff it out and relight
it if you wish. When you feel the spell is complete, or the candle is
spent, discard it and return the plant materials to nature—but keep
one reminder on your altar of the greatness of the tree. This could
be a branch, leaf, piece of bark, or a seed or nut.

Reference

Darwin, Charles. *The Origin of Species*. Vol 2. New York: P. F.
    Collier & Son, 1909.

Beltane Ritual

Suzanne Ress

THIS BELTANE RITUAL IS best done outdoors with a close-knit group of individuals. If the weather is unpleasant or you are a solitary practitioner, feel free to modify it as necessary.

The Red Fruit of Joy

Before the evening of April 30, you'll need to prepare a few things for this group ritual. You'll need a Green Man mask—be as creative as you like with it. An easy way to make one is to glue artificial oak leaves all over a simple green, brown, or gold eye mask. You can do something much more elaborate if you are so inclined, from a whole-face to whole-head-covering mask, purchased or handmade, with real or artificial greenery.

You'll need a wreath of spring flowers. Ideally, the flowers should be fresh lilacs, lily of the valley, and hawthorn blossoms, but other kinds will do, as will artificial ones. The flower colors should be white, blue, purple, and yellow. They can simply be attached to a wire head-sized circle with pipe cleaners or, as with the mask, feel free to create something much fancier.

The ritual is best done in an open space with, optimally, a large oak tree to oversee. Two bonfires should be made with at least six feet between them. If you are unable to build open bonfires legally and safely, white pillar candles can stand in for them. If you do not have access to an open space with a large oak tree, obtain several acorns and a wand or stick of oak wood.

You will need a bowl full of red fruit. Strawberries are the best but, in case of allergy or other reasons making strawberries impossible, you may use cherries, red apples, or red grapes.

You will need a bottle of red wine or, if preferred, red fruit juice and a beautiful goblet in glass or silver.

Prepare your altar and bonfires, if you will be using them, ahead of time. If you are permitted and desirous of using bonfires, gather up your wood, kindling, and lighters in two safe locations, side-by-side, with at least six feet between them—wide enough a space for people to move between them safely.

If you are using pillar candles to represent bonfires, make sure you have lanterns or hurricane lamps to contain them in; otherwise, even an imperceptible breeze will blow them out. You can use as few as two of them or as many as you can afford! These can be set on tables or directly on the ground. Make sure there is no dry organic material near them that could accidentally catch fire.

Make an altar facing north, facing and balanced evenly between the two bonfires, at least six feet away from them. On the altar, place the Green Man mask, the wreath of spring flowers, the bowl of red fruit, the wine or juice, the oak stick or wand and acorns, and any other items, such as ritual jewelry, potion bottles, magic coins, amulets, etc., you wish to consecrate and charge.

The bonfires or candles should be lit at moonrise on April 30. It is important that this ritual is held outdoors, but if it is raining or the weather is otherwise inclement, the ritual may be held under a portico, a covered deck, or perhaps inside an open garage (no bonfires, obviously!). At the very least, open up all the windows in your indoor locale so that fresh air may circulate.

When all participants are ready and the bonfires or candles have been lit, the leader shall lift the oak stick or wand in her left hand and create a magical enclosure by leading all participants in walking deosil around and between the bonfires and the altar to form the shape of a three-leaved clover. Participants may drum, chant, ring bells, shake maracas, or just meditate as they walk the clover many times over and over. This will draw in fairies and magic and close out any negative forces, as well as raise the group's collective energy to a crescendo.

After enough time has elapsed, and the group's energy level is very fine and focused, the noise and movement should be halted by the coven leader by returning to the altar and raising her wand or stick. She will then select two people to represent the Green Man and the Great Mother. These two will come forward and stand before the altar with the bonfires to their backs. The flower wreath will be placed upon the Great Mother's head, and these words spoken by the coven's leader:

You stand before us wreathed in flowers, immortal and perfect, the mother of all earth.

The mask shall be put on the Green Man's face, and the following words uttered:

You stand here covered in green leaves, the spirit of renewal and joy.

Take a few moments to feel the presence of the Great Mother through this representative human.

Now the Green Man and the Great Mother turn to each other and take each other's hands, and the leader says:

Joined together, spirit and body, you will reach ecstatic pleasure, ensuring fertility and new life and spirit for all here present.

Take some moments for the Green Man's joyous presence to be felt and appreciated.

Now the two shall dance and skip along the clover path previously marked out, singing, shouting, laughing, or remaining silent, as they see fit. Others of the group may drum, play their various instruments, or vocalize, as desired. After a short time, the remainder of the participants will join in the dance, following the two lovers, faster and faster around the three-leaf clover, until everyone has had enough.

Then, still inside the magic dome, the leader shall return to the altar and present the bowl of strawberries to the fairies and other beneficial spirits present, who shall eat some of it first, and only after they have eaten their fill shall the human and god-representative participants enjoy some for themselves.

The leader will say:

All eat now of the bountiful red fruit. Let the sweet juices of fairy spittle and fertility, and all of earth's creativity, enter into you.

The red wine shall be poured into the goblet. The leader will bless this with her wand and say:

All partake of the red libation, its earthly goodness bringing joy to our spirits.

First the fairies and then each human person shall drink some of it.

Taking the acorns into her right hand and tapping them with the oak stick or wand, the leader will say:

Overseen by the great oak, king of trees, may all of us here, visible and invisible, take pleasure in the continuing productivity and ever-renewed beauty offered by the Great Mother and celebrate her union with the Green Man. Go forth all, in happiness and in peace.

At this point in the ritual, if there are items to be charged, now is the time.

To reopen the magic dome, the leader will walk the clover widdershins and backwards three times. And now, all may partake of whatever other refreshments there may be, or they may dance, or relax, or lie down upon the earth, or converse with the fairies or with one another, or walk amongst the trees until they are exhausted or until the dawn of May 1, whichever comes sooner.

Notes

Notes

Litha

A Time of Illumination

Blake Octavian Blair

THE SUMMER SOLSTICE, also called Midsummer, Litha, and Alban Hefin, is the time we celebrate the peak of the sun's power and the longest day of the year. Many revel in the summer's long days, which often include a sense of being energized and renewed. However, spiritually there is a lot more to celebrate, even if you're not a "sun baby." The Summer Solstice is a time of illumination where we have an opportunity to better see the unseen. We tap into this energetic current and see into ourselves and the otherworlds.

With the sun at the height of its power, you may or may not be celebrating the vast hours of daylight. If you are, wonderful, enjoy this special time! If you are not, don't worry. I'm not much of a fan of the long days myself. In fact, I tend to thrive in the dark half of the year. So why in the world would I be the one to write about celebrating the sabbat celebrating all things solar? Because I do love other solar aspects of this day. In fact, the more I tap into the day beyond its literal celebration of heat and light, and more into its mystical and energetic qualities of light and illumination, the more I really connect to the celebration of this sabbat. There is something for us all at this powerful time.

We actually derive the word solstice from the Latin *solstitium*, essentially meaning "sun stands still." For a few days at the Summer Solstice, the sun appears to stand still in its course, creating a sort of pause and between-time. This provides us a great opportunity to stop and reflect upon ourselves in this vast illuminating light. With the sun at the height of its power and illuminating the view between worlds, the veil is seen to be thin between our apparent world and that of the otherworld. We can peer into the depths of ourselves as well as into other realities. In fact, the tradition of fairy lore revolving around this time is rich.

Litha is not often highlighted as a time of introspection, with other sabbats in the dark half of the year getting more press in that department, despite Summer Solstice being a perfect time. We can take this time to utilize the extra daylight for doing ritual work in the glowing solar energy and also to harness the qualities of energetic illumination to look within ourselves and see with an increased clarity where we have grown and what our strengths are, and to get an honest assessment of where we have improved personally as well as where we have room for improvement. Perhaps we have weaknesses that can be identified as areas that provide room for growth and improvement. Truthfully, that is what weaknesses are, and it's much more constructive and less self-depreciating to affirm that you can improve on something than to see it as a permanent deficit! Meditate upon illuminating ways you can use your strengths to help fortify you in your weak areas. This time of active solar energy is good to break out of any passivity that may have prevented you from taking action in the past and develop an action plan to move forward! This is also something that, if desired, groups can undertake too. It can be a great time to set new practices and plans into motion for groves, covens, and other groups as well.

Whenever we are in our own element, utilizing and having our strengths highlighted, or are acting from a place of truly being comfortable with ourselves, people often say we are "shining." So, perhaps the shining solar radiance of Litha can help us out. We shine best when we are living authentically as ourselves, and the first step to that is being honest with ourselves about who we are—the good and the bad. Nobody is perfect, and we all have room for improvement.

However, the window into the inner workings of ourselves and the communities we are a part of is not the only thing illuminated by the height of our celestial solar powerhouse … there are other beings afoot too. The veil is thin, and the fair folk are afoot.

Many people are feeling playful and jubilant at Midsummer gatherings, and the vibe can be absolutely infectious. However, I'd like to posit that you might well be riding more than the wave of the energies of your fellow human comrades. Summer Solstice is also a time of fairy raids. What is a fairy raid you may ask? A grand parade-like procession of fairies, and Midsummer is a fit time for such occasions. Tales of fairy raids report that they have all the pomp and circumstance you might imagine with horse-drawn carriages and all the fanfare one might expect for potential fairy royalty. With the veil thin, many can perceive the jubilation of the fairies as our realms bleed together for a time.

However, one must not forget that actual fairies are not, on the whole, the miniature pixie-like creatures that have been rolled in glitter by modern culture. Fairies come in all sizes and temperaments, many of them not the most innocent toward humans. To say the least, they can be tricksters and, in fact, have their own moral code of which it could take an entire volume of its own to discuss. However, there are precautions one might wish to take (which can luckily be rolled into the festivities) while enjoying a hopefully peaceful coexistence with the fair folk during this radiant and jubilant solar celebration. Iron is a longstanding material that provides protection and keeps potential marauding fairies at bay. This is one of the many reasons that there is a tradition of using iron horseshoes above doorways. If you feel a concern for fairy mischief, maybe it is time to hang a few. On second thought, perhaps if you're engaging in some lawn games during the long daylight and celebrations, when playing a friendly game of horseshoes, perhaps see to it you're using authentic iron shoes in your tossing.

However, not all the fair folk are necessarily out to cause a ruckus in your celebrations, and it would certainly be in good measure to leave some offerings to be on their good side. One of the traditional offerings to the good folk, honey, is especially fitting for this solar celebration. Honey itself, with its rich golden color and its most magical production by the mystical bee, has longstanding solar associations and is associated with the fire element. Leaving the fair folk offerings as part of your Litha rites is not a horrible idea. Also, using a euphemism to refer to them to avoid any offense or undue attention is traditional. One such euphemism for the fairy is "the good neighbors." Perhaps, by trying to be a good neighbor yourself and leaving offerings for them, you can avoid troublesome behavior on their part.

While we are being mindful of our otherworldly neighbors at our Midsummer celebrations and their potential benevolence or marauding trickery, it is important to remember we have the potential for the same. Under this time of illumination, perhaps we need to realize that we are in fact human, and like the fair folk, we are a mixed lot. We humans are capable of bizarre viewpoints on ethics and engaging in what would be considered less than admirable behavior. However, we are also capable of honorable and benevolent behaviors. So as we engage in a little bit of good faith and neighborly relations leaving offerings for the fey, we can go a little less hard on ourselves. We can use powerful illuminating qualities of the sun to plunge into the depths of ourselves and our relations to fellow humans and other forms of life of all kinds.

How we humans behave as a species, we are finding, has a profound impact on other species. This is readily evident in the catastrophic effects of climate change. At this time of the height of the sun's path, it is easy to see illuminated the abundance of life we are interconnected with in the web of being. Anthropocentric viewpoints are both dangerous and easy to fall into. We should take care to realize we are but one species upon an earth teeming with diverse life forms. We are not superior to any other. Flowers are in bloom, bees are buzzing about from plant to plant, the trees are lush and green, the birds are about, and if we are up at dawn and dusk there are a host of wonderful crepuscular animal activities we might bear witness to. This, of course, is only the tip of the iceberg. Well, the iceberg may not be there for long, both literally and metaphorically, if we don't examine our ways. It's important to remember, whether we are fans of summer heat or not, that the sun and our planet's relation to it are vital to sustaining life on our planet. It's important to remember that rising global temperatures, which result in melting sea ice at the poles and other devastating effects attributed to climate change, are not the fault of the sun but, rather, results of complicated chain reactions set off in large contribution from human actions, including the burning of fossil fuels on mass and industrial scales. The sun's sacred light and its powerful heat, when we work in harmony with the natural world, actually provide the nourishment and conditions needed to grow the agricultural bounty of fresh fruits and vegetables we celebrate as part of our festival menus as the Wheel of the Year turns. What is a festival without a feast? Remember as you sit down to your sabbat meal to give thanks to the divine power of the sun for helping to bring the food before you.

With the celebration of light, life, and the fiery power of the sun, it is no wonder that bonfires are a traditional part of Litha celebrations. The fire at Summer Solstice really takes on the role of mirroring for us the flames of the fiery star that brings us life. This fire without resonates with the mirroring fires within our souls. This forms a sacred triad of flames among the flames of the sun, the solstice ritual fire, and the spiritual fire within us. Illumination abounds in this time of peak daylight and solar celebration!

References

Daimler, Morgan. *A New Dictionary of Fairies: A 21st Century Exploration of Celtic and Related Western European Fairies.* Winchester, UK/Washington, USA: Moon Books, 2020.

Evans-Wentz, W. Y. *The Fairy Faith in Celtic Countries: The Classic Study of Leprechauns, Pixies, and Other Fairy Spirits.* New York, New York: Kensington Publishing Corp. 1994, 1996.

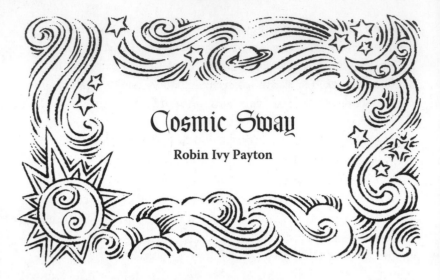

Cosmic Sway

Robin Ivy Payton

ON JUNE 21, the Sun moves into Cancer, marking the astrological shift from spring to summer. The Moon will be in Aries, waning after the Sagittarius Full Moon on June 14. Both Sagittarius and Aries are signs of fire, intensifying action, activity, movement, and heat during this celebration of the Sun. Waning Moon in Aries is a time of weeding out and cleansing by fire to prepare for expansion and beginnings ahead. This particular solstice is therefore well suited to using fire as a means for letting go, and to flames that are carefully and thoughtfully controlled. The abundance of heat energy in this part of the lunar cycle should be considered when engaging in all rituals involving fire, from the tiniest candle to largest bonfire.

Jupiter and Mars will also be traveling the degrees of Aries on solstice 2022. Jupiter indicates the big picture, a broadening of perspective, changes, and initiations related to education, travel, business, and growing in wisdom. Mars, the warrior planet, is at home in Aries, encouraging action and pushing the limits. Astrologically, there's a sense of confronting problems or issues and taking bold steps into new territory during this time of year. Themes include breaking down barriers or destroying paradigms in order to recreate ones that are stronger, fiercer, and more suited to present times.

With the Moon close to Jupiter on the solstice, personal growth, preparing for beginnings, sense of self, and independence are naturally highlighted. As part of your celebration this year, acknowledge what you're burning away. Both planets are direct in motion, aligning with progress, momentum, and sense of forward direction.

Loving Venus

A few heavenly bodies will be retrograde on this year's solstice. Saturn, Neptune, Pluto, and the North Node travel many months in retrograde. Venus influences us with a shorter, and often more personally impactful, retrograde, while happily situated in sensual Taurus, one of her zodiac homes. Representing love, sex, beauty, and abundance during this cycle, Venus aligns with Pluto in Capricorn, each at 28 degrees of these earthy, physical signs. Notice stirring emotions and realizations in the relationship realm. Often Venus and Pluto combine forces to bring transformation and rebirth. Awakening desire, opening to intimacy, and blending physical, emotional, and soulful aspects of love are some results of our Venus-Pluto trine. Venus is soft and receptive, the voice or soundtrack playing continuously as our life experiences unfold. Pluto resides, often subtle in the depths, waiting to be roused by something such as touch, sight, or sound, triggered like a memory or recollection of a dream.

In harmony during this solstice, this duo speaks to and through our heartfelt relationships and innermost feelings. Venus aligned with romantic Neptune two days prior and shares sparks with Jupiter during the June 28 New Moon. The planet of love appears to be connecting soulmates and fulfilling dreams as the Sun burns high in the sky.

Astrological Activities

Depending where you live and what your community is like, there are many ways to honor the solstice. Beginning in the morning, travel or face east to see the sun rise. Invoke the direction of the east and all its creatures and plants, and any other associations you have with the east. Recognize solar animals, like Eagle, Hawk, Swan, and Horse. You may also visualize creatures of the water, such as seals, and any other animal life special and unique to you.

Sun salutations are a physical way to open to the Sun, feel your strength, and increase your life force. Remember to breathe well as you move, first raising arms and open hands to the sky as you breathe in, and folding forward gently toward the earth with head and hands as you exhale. Salutations can be as simple as this, repeating the upward and downward flow, or other postures like planks, backbends, and downward dogs can be added for a yoga-style Sun A salute. Greet the season and yourself with gratitude and joy.

Use fire and smoke as a way of cleansing and releasing during this waning Moon. At sunrise or sunset, light a bundle of sage or mugwort and burn until there are glowing embers. Gently blow on the flame to diminish it, then sage around your body, shaking the bundle safely around you or someone else. (Be very careful around hair and clothing. You needn't get too close to skin or hair to receive the clearing.) Working with mugwort is said to stimulate dreams.

Meditate on your tarot cards during solstice. Ace and Page of Wands align with both the fire energy of peak Sun and with this year's Moon in Aries, the first fire sign. The Chariot, long associated with the Sun's journey into Cancer, and the Sun card, representing youth, are also cards of Litha. On your altar or windowsill, set up your solstice spell to invite the energy and vitality of this season. Crystals such as citrine, yellow calcite, or perhaps some rose quartz for the heart enhance your spell. Understand your own intentions at Midsummer and clarify any release you are approaching as you cross this threshold.

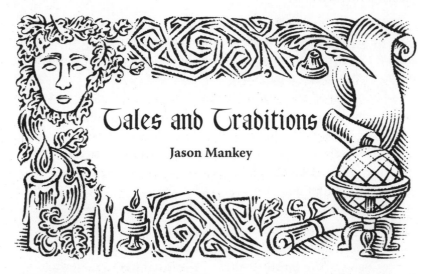

Tales and Traditions

Jason Mankey

WHILE THE RITUALS OF Witchcraft are most readily associated with the moon and the darkness of night, at Litha the sun takes center stage! Litha is a celebration of the sun at the peak of its power, and celebrations of the Summer Solstice are among the oldest spiritual traditions in the history of humanity. Even older than solstice celebrations are traditions and customs that venerate and honor the sun. Many of these practices are still honored today on or near the Summer Solstice and have histories that go back possibly thousands of years.

Litha: Summer Sun and Fires Keep On Burning

As a round disc, the sun has been interpreted as both an eye and a wheel over the millennia. Perhaps the eye is the most obvious and implies that the sun sees all and knows all, especially in the light of day. For this reason, many solar and sky deities were described as "all knowing" and "all seeing." While the sun's amount of time in the sky waxes and wanes across the year, it generally remains a daily visitor in most places. For this reason, people also made oaths to the sun. Who better to swear to than the one presence (or deity) that's always watching you?

Due to the movement of the sun, many ancient people saw the sun as a wheel. Even the most unobservant person is aware that the sun is in constant motion throughout the day, so why not symbolize the sun as something that implies movement? The sun as a wheel could then be pulled along by a goddess or god (sun goddesses were nearly as prominent in the ancient world as sun gods!), a team of horses, or a deity steering their chariot. The symbolism of the sun being drawn through the sky by a chariot became so common that the spoked wheel of the solar chariot became a popular image on coins, pottery, and statues.

The solar wheel was also honored in a very literal sense closer to the ground by people building large wooden wheels, lighting them on fire, and rolling them down hills. The first reference to such activities dates to the fourth century CE and is directly connected to ancient Paganism. In the *Acts of the Martyr St. Vincent* the author mentions a group of French Pagans rolling a burning wheel down a hill into a river. At the conclusion of the wheel's journey the pieces were picked up and reassembled in the temple of a sky-god. The author who chronicled the life of Saint Vincent didn't specify what time of year the French Pagans rolled their wheel, but it might have very well been near the Summer Solstice. An English monk writing one-thousand years later mentions a similar wheel, but this time with a date, Saint John's Eve, the start of Midsummer, the celebration of the Summer Solstice (Hutton 1996, 311).

Writing less than two hundred years later, the German theologian Thomas Naogeorgus writes about how common flaming wheels were on Midsummer, and includes a description of their use:

> *Some others had gotten a rotten wheel, all worn and cast aside*
> *Which they covered round with straw and rope, they closely hide;*
> *And carried to some mountain's top, all with fire alight,*

They hurled it down with violence, what dark became the night:
Resembling much the sun, that from the heavens down should fall,
A strange and monstrous sight it seems, and fearful to them all.

(Hampson 1841, 301, emphasis in original, old English cleaned up by Mankey.)

Here the solar wheel is explicitly linked to the sun, implying that the churchman who wrote this passage was well aware of the burning wheel's connection to Paganism.

A similar account published in 1909 documents a similar practice in England that allegedly dates from the 1820s. This account has people running down a hill with the wheel, holding the flaming wheel upward by inserting a pole through the middle of it. This particular account has an extra bit of folklore attached to it. Just how long the wheel stayed on fire as it rolled was said to predict how that year's crops would turn out. If the wheel's fire went out before it reached the bottom of the hill, it was thought that the harvest would be poor (Hutton 1996, 311).

Flaming wheels are probably not allowed where most of us live, but bonfires have been a summer solstice staple for thousands of years and are another way to symbolize the sun. In many parts of Europe, it's still common for bonfires to be lit on Saint John's Night (or Eve), the successor to Pagan Summer Solstice traditions. Most of those fires primarily burned wood, but an English monk writing during the 1300s observed that some Midsummer fires were composed primarily of bones. According to the monk, the burning bones were a dragon repellent (Hutton 1996, 312–313). In other parts of Europe, it was thought that bonfires kept malicious Witches at bay. The very word bonfire probably derives from "banefire," a fire lit to drive away evil forces and energies.

Both fire and the rays of the sun are seen as purifying, an association that dates back to the Pagan past. Writing in the first century CE, the Roman writer Pliny the Elder mentions the purifying power of smoke and encouraged farmers to set up bonfires around their crops as a form of protection. In later centuries, similar ideas would lead to people taking smoking brands from the Midsummer bonfire and running through their fields with them, to keep the crops free from blight and supernatural forces.

Jumping over a Midsummer night's bonfire (or its ashes) was considered good luck in many societies, with some groups taking this to the extreme. An account from the middle of the nineteenth century in Ireland has young men jumping through the flames of a bonfire forward and backward to celebrate the solstice. It was also believed that whoever braved the most intense flames would have the most power over evil. As the night progressed, and the fire grew less intense, others would leap or walk through it. Young unmarried women who leaped through the fire three times back and forth were assured a speedy marriage and many children (Hutton 1996, 319–320).

Our ancestors honored and praised the sun with flaming wheels, smoke, and bonfires, honoring the power of fire on the longest day of the year. Today many of us are not in a position to light much more than a grill or a candle in our backyards (large fires, and certainly flaming wheels are against the law in many areas for safety reasons), but we can still celebrate the sun just as they did. Hail the fiery disc that watches over us all!

References

Hampson, R. T. *Medii Ævi Kalendarium: Or Dates, Charters, And Customs of the Middle Ages [...]*. Vol. 1. London: Henry Kent Causton and Company, 1841.

Hutton, Ronald. *Blood and Mistletoe: The History of the Druids in Britain*. New Haven, CT: Yale University Press, 2009.

———. *The Stations of the Sun: A History of the Ritual Year in Britain*. Oxford: Oxford University Press, 1996.

Mankey, Jason. *Witch's Wheel of the Year: Rituals for Circles, Solitaries & Covens*. Woodbury, MN: Llewellyn Publications, 2019.

Feasts and Treats

Elizabeth Barrette

LITHA CELEBRATES THE SUN at the height of its power during the Summer Solstice. This is the peak of the growing season, when everything is green and gardens are overflowing with summer produce. Life and light are at their zenith, with death and darkness far away. It's a popular time for outdoor parties and picnics too. That calls for food that can stand up to summer heat.

Stuffed Strawberries

Strawberries are a quintessential June treat, representing love and fertility. Fresh mint nicely mimics the leafy green top of a strawberry, creating an edible garnish.

Prep time: 30 minutes
Inactive: 30 minutes or more
Servings: about 12

1 pint fresh strawberries
zest of 1 lemon
juice of ½ lemon (about 1½ tablespoons)
1 (8 ounce) package full-fat cream cheese, softened
¼ cup mascarpone cheese
¼ cup powdered sugar

1 teaspoon vanilla extract
1 handful fresh mint

Set out the cream cheese to soften at room temperature.

Rinse and pat dry the strawberries. Pull off the leaves and use a paring knife to remove the stems, opening the core of the strawberries.

Zest a lemon. Cut it in half and juice one half. Save the zest and juice in a small bowl.

In a medium mixing bowl, combine 1 package softened full-fat cream cheese, ¼ cup mascarpone cheese, and ¼ cup powdered sugar. Mix in the lemon zest and juice. Add 1 teaspoon vanilla extract and mix until smooth.

Put the cream cheese filling into a plastic baggie and snip off one corner. Squeeze the filling into each strawberry.

Remove the mint leaves from the stems, discarding any damaged leaves. Poke a mint leaf into the top of each strawberry. Arrange the strawberries on a platter and chill in the refrigerator for at least half an hour before serving.

Heirloom Tomato Toss

Tomatoes are the epitome of summer. They reach their peak in the long hours of the sun. These sweet, juicy vegetables are best enjoyed fresh right now. Unlike modern hybrids, these "heirloom" or "antique" cultivars are open-pollinated and selected for intense flavor rather than shipping convenience. They come in many fascinating sizes, shapes, and colors. Red, orange, yellow, and pink symbolize the sun but there are also green, purple, brown, white, and almost black ones!

Prep time: 15–20 minutes
Servings: 6 (1 cup) or 12 (½ cup)

4 pounds of heirloom tomatoes
1 bunch of Italian sweet basil (about 1 cup)
6 tablespoons full-flavor extra-virgin olive oil

2 tablespoons balsamic vinegar
2 cloves of garlic
1 tablespoon sweet marjoram
1 teaspoon oregano
1 teaspoon thyme
½ teaspoon rosemary
½ teaspoon sage
½ teaspoon cracked green pepper
½ teaspoon fleur de sel or sea salt

Rinse and pat dry 4 pounds of heirloom tomatoes. Remove the stems and cores. Grape tomatoes and small cherry tomatoes should be cut in half. Larger cherry tomatoes may need to be cut in quarters. Beefsteaks and other full-size tomatoes should be diced. First slice them, then cut the slices into strips, then cut the strips into cubes. Just roughly chopping them won't make a tidy salad. If some of the tomatoes have large amounts of slime inside, remove it and use the firm parts. Put the tomato bits into a big salad bowl.

Rinse and pat dry 1 bunch of Italian sweet basil. Remove the stems and large veins by tearing the leaf sides away from the middle. Tear the leaves into bite-sized pieces; you should have about a cup. Put the torn basil in a bowl.

Make the dressing in a clean jar with a lid. First, pour in 6 tablespoons full-flavor extra-virgin olive oil. (If you have olive oil infused with any of the herbs in this recipe, you can use that.) Add 2 tablespoons balsamic vinegar.

Peel and mince 2 cloves of garlic. Add them to the jar of dressing. Add 1 tablespoon sweet marjoram, 1 teaspoon oregano, 1 teaspoon thyme, ½ teaspoon rosemary, ½ teaspoon sage, and ½ teaspoon cracked green pepper.

Put the lid on the jar snugly. Shake briefly to combine all the ingredients. This is not an emulsified vinaigrette, so you're not trying to make a smooth blend, just distribute the ingredients equally.

Add the basil leaves to the tomato bits in the salad bowl and toss to combine. Shake the dressing one last time and pour it slowly over the salad, tossing as you go. Finally, sprinkle ½ teaspoon fleur de sel over the salad.

Serve immediately. This recipe makes about 6 (1-cup) servings as a bowl salad or (12 ½-cup) servings as a side dish.

Note: In addition to standing on its own as a salad, the Heirloom Tomato Toss also makes an excellent topping for sandwiches, baked potatoes, tacos, chili, and so on. Use it for extra flavor anywhere that you would use diced tomatoes. If you like a leafier salad, put a scoop of this on top of Romaine lettuce or baby spinach.

Rosewater Lemonade

Nothing says summer like pink lemonade. This recipe adds a few extra ingredients to make it more magical. Strawberries add sweetness and color. Rose petals and rosewater evoke love and luxury. Lemons refresh and uplift the mood, standing for the yellow sun at the height of its power.

Prep time: 5 minutes for ice cubes, plus 10 minutes for lemonade
Inactive: 5 hours for ice cubes
Servings: 4

fresh rose petals
water
4 cups water
4 lemons
½ cup strawberries
½ cup sugar
1 tablespoon dried rose petals
1–2 teaspoons rosewater
½ cup ice

Ice Cubes

Into an ice cube tray, pour enough water to cover the bottom of each cubicle. Place in the freezer until the surface frosts over, about half an hour.

Wet the fresh rose petals, then place one rose petal into each cubicle, pressing down to contact the ice. Return the tray to the freezer for half an hour.

Fill the cubicles to the brim with water. Return the tray to the freezer until frozen solid, about 5 hours.

Lemonade

Put 4 cups of water into a high-speed blender.

Peel the lemons. Remove any seeds. Put the sections in the blender.

Rinse the strawberries and cut off the tops. Add the strawberries to the blender.

Add ½ cup sugar and 1 tablespoon dried rose petals. Add 1 teaspoon of rosewater, then taste. You should get just a hint of rose flavor; too much and it tastes soapy. Add another teaspoon if needed.

Put in ½ cup regular ice.

Use the "smoothie" setting, or process until liquefied. If you want pulp-free lemonade, strain it before pouring into glasses. Serve over rose petal ice cubes.

Store in the refrigerator for up to a year or tuck into the freezer. If you're a home canner, process in a water bath canner for longer storage.

To serve, add two or three tablespoonfuls of shrub to a glass of chopped ice and water. There's nothing more refreshing on a hot summer day!

Crafty Crafts

Charlie Rainbow Wolf

Litha, or Midsummer, marks the middle of the summer (in the Northern Hemisphere) and the time of year where the nights are at their shortest. It's the apex of the sun's revolution; everything is growing like mad. It's the time of fetes and festivals, and when the Oak King rules.

It's also a time when there's some urgency to start getting things accomplished before winter. As the sun peaks, it whispers the long dark nights are on their way again. The Oak King will soon surrender to the Holly King; the cycle continues.

Melt and Pour Soap

What better way to relax after a long day out in the sun than to take a soothing shower or recline in a beautiful bath? The melt-and-pour method of soapmaking is quick and easy. It's also a good way to use up the little scraps of soap that linger in the soap dish. My mum-in-law taught me that; she kept these scraps in a jar on her old Aga stove, and when the jar was full, she would mix the soft soap together then tip it into a container to harden into a bar again.

Materials

Soap: For small batches, I favor castile soaps, usually available from grocery stores or online retailers. If you plan on making soap regularly, consider bulk-buying the soap base from a specialist supplier. Hobby and craft shops offer something between the two; not bulk, but enough soap base to make several bars.

Mold: Soap molds are fun! They're reusable and affordable, and available from most places that sell the soap base. No mold? No problem. Use an old yogurt pot or the bottom of a plastic jar. The bottom of a pop bottle makes a great mold, because the uneven bottom turns the soap into a massage bar. I favour the silicon molds; it's easy to get the soap out of them.

Glass jug

Pan

Spoon (one that you won't be using for food)

Something to grate the soap: Some soapmakers use an old food processor, some a cheese grater; I just use an old knife.

Fragrance oil (optional): I use essential oils in my soap, but fragrance oils are acceptable and often less expensive. Make sure they are safe to use in soap. Some fragrance oils are only suitable for candles.

Colorant (optional): Commercial food colorings might discolor over time. There are colorants specifically made for soap and bath products. My favorite is clay; various clays add different properties to the soap and give it a lovely natural hue.

Cost: A bar of castile soap is less than $3 most places; buying in bulk is cheaper per bar but initially more expensive. A silicone soap mold with multiple cavities for more than one bar of soap is around $5. If you want to invest in soap molds, fragrance oils, herbs, colorants, or other inclusions, the sky's the limit as to how much you will need to spend. Lavender oil is readily available and inexpensive and goes well with purple Brazilian clay—the clay is $5 or so an ounce and a little goes a long way. Any old knife you have on hand to grate the soap will do; you don't need to use a food processor or even a cheese grater.

Time spent: It doesn't take long at all to melt and pour the soap, but it's best to let it cure overnight before it is used.

Lather Up!

Cover the work surface with old paper, particularly if coloring will be used. Finely slice the soap into small cubes or slivers and put them in the glass jug. Put the glass jug in the pan of gently simmering water. The soap should melt fairly easily, especially if it is a designated melt-and-pour soap base.

Once the soap is melted (give it a thorough stir to ensure there are no lumps), add the fragrance oil and colorant. The strength of both is a matter of personal choice, but go lightly—it cannot be removed once it's been added. I usually use about 4 drops of oil to 1 bar of soap and add the coloring bit by bit until I get the pastel shade I'm seeking.

Pour the soap into the mold. Let it set somewhere cool for at least two hours before removing it—overnight is better. The smaller the mold, the quicker the soap will set. I've found it easier to remove soap from silicone molds than the harder plastic ones, but neither is difficult.

Once you're familiar with the process, it's possible to add all kinds of inclusions to the soaps. Oatmeal makes a nice exfoliant; for a harsher texture, ground seeds and nuts might be added. Some herbs and flowers—sage or marigold, for example—work well when added to the soap; others—like lavender or rose—tend to go a funky color after a few days, which won't harm the soap, but it could look ugly. Mostly it's best to sprinkle dried flowers and herbs on the top of the bar as it's setting. Have fun with this and experiment; it's good clean fun!

Suppliers
JOANN and Michaels are craft shops that have both a physical and
   an online presence.
Brambleberry.com and bulkapothecary.com are online suppliers of
   bulk materials.

Further Reading
Melt & Pour Soapmaking by Marie Browning, 2001.
Melt & Mold Soap Crafting by C. Kaila Westerman, 2000.
The Joy of Melt and Pour Soap Crafting by Lisa Maliga, 2011.

Candle Magic

Ember Grant

FOR THE SUMMER SOLSTICE, here are two spells that utilize candles with mirrors. In honor of the longest day, we celebrate the sun's strength; soon it will begin to wane. For now, let's revel in the light of both fire and sunshine.

Healing Light

For this spell, you need a small pocket mirror you can carry—a compact is ideal, but any small mirror will do. In addition, you'll need enough candles to make a circle around the mirror. You can use any size or number of candles you wish, but try to use white, yellow, orange, or red—or a combination of these colors. If you wish, carve sun symbols into the candles.

Your goal is to charge the mirror with both sunlight and candlelight and then use the mirror as a symbol for healing light. Imagine the mirror as a battery. You'll charge it with both candlelight and sunlight. Imagine both types of light as healing fire—the candle flames and the radiant light of the sun. Harness both into the mirror. Every time you look into it, visualize that healing light reflects back to you.

You can do this in whatever order you choose—sunlight first, then candles, or candles, then sunlight the next day. Place the mirror outside in full midday sunshine. Leave it there for at least one hour. Do this on the summer solstice or any bright day. Visualize that you're capturing the light—this is one reason a compact works well because you can close it, figuratively capturing the light. For the nighttime portion of the spell, open the mirror in a dimly lit area and light the candles in a circle around the mirror. Let the candles burn out.

Any time you look at your reflection in that mirror, imagine the sunlight and candle flames and chant:

Sun and fire, day and night, in this glass I hold your light;
healing rays of summer days, bring magic when it's in my sight.

Visualize the light flowing through you with energizing, healing power.

Radiance Spell

Summer represents the full bloom of life, a flourishing, vigorous time. No matter what your age, this spell is intended to help you channel the full splendor of a beautiful summer—the magic of warm evenings, fireflies, lush trees, and cool water. If seasons are life, then summer is the height—be your summer self, your most strong and beautiful inside and out. Embrace the fullness of life wherever you are. You are radiant.

For this spell, you will need a large mirror, such as one you may have in your bathroom or bedroom—one that lets you see as much of yourself as possible.

You will need three candles of any size or color, but make sure that you can hold one of them comfortably in your hands without burning yourself. (Use a container if necessary.) You will hold one candle as you stand in front of the mirror and place the other two on each side of you on a counter, table, or dresser. Try to catch the light of the candles in the mirror with you, if possible.

Light the candles and, as you view your reflection, say these words:

Let the flames of candles three
show the traits that flatter me;
inner beauty brought to light—
I'm radiant and shining bright.

Stand or sit that way as long as you can. Meditate on you—your inner and outer beauty. Feel it. See it. Shine with the radiance of self-love. Reflect on who you are and who you want to be. Are you your best self? If not, why? What changes would you like to make? Take time to reflect on more than what you see, but how you feel. Know that you have the power to be your best self.

When you're finished with your self-reflection, extinguish the candles or keep them burning as long as you wish. Keep using them for this purpose over time until they burn out.

Simple Midsummer Protection Spell

Ancient people all over Europe are known to have celebrated Midsummer. According to scholar Ronald Hutton, Midsummer (as well as Midwinter) celebrations were common throughout ancient Britain and almost certainly employed fire. There is evidence of "the making of sacred fires at the opening of summer and at its solstice, to bless and protect people and their livestock from the dangers of the season" (Hutton 2013, loc 7698). Fire was used to purify with smoke, and to provide protection.

Use a red votive candle and carve it with protective symbols such as pentagrams. Imagine ancient tribes of people at Midsummer creating protective fires for their livestock and villages. You are connecting with your ancestors and all those who came before by utilizing the power of fire, even if you're merely lighting a candle. The fire is symbolic. It is pure power. As you light the candle, visualize the element of fire forming a protective shield around you that deflects all negative energy and harm of any kind. You can imagine a circle of fire, a series of fires in a ring around you, or a sphere of fire that encompasses you like a ball. Even though fire can destroy, in this case it's warding all harm away from you. Say these words three times:

Fire is power, and it's mine to wield; fire is power, and it is my shield.

Allow the candle to burn out. Anytime you need to evoke the protective shield, repeat the phrase and visualization.

Reference

Hutton, Ronald. *Pagan Britain*. Yale University Press: New Haven and London. Kindle edition, 2013.

Litha Ritual

Blake Octavian Blair

LITHA, OR MIDSUMMER, also referred to as Alban Hefin in the Druid tradition, is a joyous time of celebration of the height of the sun's power. Summer Solstice jubilation abounds! However, we should not forget to make friends with our otherworldly neighbors at this time when our worlds collide.

Offerings and Illumination Between the Worlds

Summer Solstice has long had associations with the fairies. At the time of Summer Solstice, the veil between this and the otherworld is especially thin, and therefore we will be having quite a bit more visitor traffic from the good neighbors than usual. Oh yes, it is to be noted that despite having done so already, it is considered a bit of a taboo to mention the fairies directly by name, as you might catch their attention and provoke undesirable results. Therefore, best to use a euphemism, as I have done in the rite itself using "the good neighbors," so as to be able to functionally mention them in a low-key yet respectful and flattering way. It is well known that the good neighbors have their own sense of morality and ethics that do not necessarily align with those of humans. An objective way to look at this is not that the good folk are immoral or unethical but rather that they have a different cultural set of morals. However, one way to help with good relations between you and the good neighbors and to avert mischief is to acknowledge them with some offerings. Milk, butter, honey, and baked goods are traditional. Sweets are often well received. This is in line with the pagan value of hospitality toward guests and visitors anyway, whether they be human or otherwise, and from this apparent world or the otherworld. Some fairy lore even states that giving the good neighbors offerings is giving them what they are owed and that not doing so would invite their wrath. So, no matter how you look at it, what better than a Litha ritual that celebrates both the height of the sun and offers hospitality and good faith to the good neighbors! When inviting people to attend your ritual, you can also invite them to bring appropriate offerings for the good neighbors.

Supplies

Offerings for the good neighbors
An altar cloth or surface (cloth on the ground, a tree stump, a flat
   stone...)
A central candle on the altar or a central fire *
Sage, incense, or other material for purification
A rattle or bell
Additional small bell(s) for use in honoring the fairies
Any other miscellaneous altar decorations or ritual tools you wish
   to have present for use.
*Practice responsible fire safety. Do check to see if there are any
   bans on open fire in your area due to fire risk. Also, practice dil-
   igent fire tending, and have a necessary fire extinguisher nearby.

Preparation

Gather the supplies listed above into a basket, backpack, or other easily transportable container for ease of location at ritual time and the journey to the ritual site. If you plan to make baked goods for offerings to the good folk, then you will want to account for the creation of these in your preparations.

Once you are at the ritual site, you'll want to first prepare your altar space with the central candle, if you choose to use one, or build the fire in a safely prepared fire pit or ring. In this case, be sure to place the fire extinguisher safely in one of the quarters (I suggest south). The candle or fire will be lit during the ritual itself. Place the offerings brought by the ritualists on or near the altar. Provide room for more to be added later. Also, place the bells that are for honoring the fairies on or near the altar at the center of the circle. Put the purification materials and the bell or rattle in the western quarter.

The ritual is written with two ritualist parts, however, it can be adapted to just one or four altogether with minor adjustments.

The Rite

Appoint two participants to stand one on either side of the western quarter of the ritual area as a gate for entry into the ritual circle. Have one burn the sage or incense and the other use the bell or rattle to ritually cleanse participants as they pass into the ritual circle. As the participants file through the gate, they then move clockwise around until choosing a place to stand in the circle. Once all participants are in the circle, you may finish creating sacred space, including calling of quarters and circlecasting, in accordance with the protocols of your tradition. Once sacred space is established, the ritualists can step forward into the center of the circle.

Ritualist 1: *We gather today in the illumination and celebration of the longest day of the year! We celebrate the height of the sun's power on this the Summer Solstice!*

Ritualist 2: *We celebrate the illumination of many things, seen and unseen, within and without, physical and ethereal, earthly and Otherwordly.*

Ritualist 1: *At this sabbat, the veil between this apparent world and the otherworld is thin. We are afforded an opportunity to see not only deep within ourselves and our earthly relationships but also across the veil between worlds. According to lore, this is a time at* which traversing between the worlds is not only possible, but many report the experience of good neighbors visiting from their otherworldly realm. Humans must be careful to not end up trapped visiting their realm. In an effort of good relations, an ounce of prevention is worth a pound of cure.

Ritualist 2: *In this case, we will present our good neighbors a variety of offerings in goodwill toward the hope that we will peacefully share the realms while the veil is thin, with no mischief between our peoples and a joyous time of celebration to be had by all! At this time, we welcome any gathered in circle here who have brought items they wish to offer the good neighbors to bring them forward and place them in the center of the circle. While doing so, please pick up one of the available bells and take your place in the circle once again.*

As this is taking place, ritualists are assisting and guiding participants as necessary.

When all participants who wish to do so have brought forth their offerings and returned to the circle, ritualist 1 proceeds.

Ritualist 1: *Now, we pause for a moment and focus on our intent of these offerings to the good neighbors. When I begin to ring my bell, please follow suit!* (Pauses for a moment or two while intent is focused. Then begins the ringing of the bells.)

Ritualist 2: *We present these gifts to the good neighbors, whether they be owed, given freely, or else-wise. May they be a gesture of our goodwill and a display of our hospitality to our good neighbors!*

Ritualist 1: *May we now, with relations between the worlds acknowledged, turn our attention to the sun, our life-giving star, and the energy it provides us both physically and metaphysically, its light and illumination.*

Ritualist 2: *Let us join in meditative communion with the sun. Close your eyes and envision yourself enveloped in the warm golden rays of the sun. Consider what the sun brings to your life, how you* *are dependent on its existence for yours. The life it brings to the earth with its light.* (Pause.)

Ritualist 1: *Picture it illuminating your body, inside and out, with radiant golden light.* (Pause.) *What is illuminated within that was once hidden.* (Pause.) *Illuminated are your strengths and weaknesses. You can see where you have grown and have room for growth.* (Pause.) *What is illuminated that you can bring to the world for the benefit of all?* (Pause.)

Ritualist 1: *Now, let us lastly consider what is revealed to us in this time of illumination about our relation to the planet, its climate, and other life upon our earth.* (Pause.)

Ritualist 2: *Open your eyes. Feel yourself rooted here again upon the grounding soil of the earth. Still illuminated in the powerful solar energy of the solstice. In peace, love, and illumination, may we move mindfully forward through many more turns of the wheel! Blessed be!*

All: *Blessed be!*

Now, in accordance with the protocols of your tradition, you can dismiss and close sacred space.

Post-Ritual Notes

It is said that any food offerings to the fairies have no value to and are not to be consumed by humans after their offering. Leave them for a time. Any offerings not consumed by nonhumans after a time may be left in nature, in a biodegradable manner (no plastics, wrappers, bottles, cans, etc.). Always leave nature as you found it. May your relations with the good neighbors be peaceful, and may you feel the blessings of solar illumination within and without during the time of Litha!

Notes

Notes

Notes

Notes

Lammas

The Sabbats as Seasons

Laura Tempest Zakroff

A PREVIOUS SUMMER NOT long ago, I was standing on top of the West Kennet Long Barrow near Avebury in England. It had been a bit of a harrowing hike and my shoes and socks were thoroughly soaked from the copious morning dew. But as I looked around, the complaints my feet were sending to my brain were hushed by the view. The sun was just gaining purchase in the startling blue morning sky. All around me, the wind gently rippled the fields of grain that surrounded the ancient burial site. The resident swallow couple went about their business, giving me a minimal side-eye as they darted around the large stones. I tried to imagine what this land looked like back during the time of the people who had built this mound. In the distance, I could see the stones and hills that had beckoned people from all around, marking Avebury as a central gathering space.

As I surveyed the beautiful landscape surrounding me, I thought, if I lived in this place, I'd definitely be celebrating the Wheel of the Year as many modern Pagans have come to know it in the last half of the century. Even Lughnasadh. How could you not feel connected to the harvest cycle with all of this beautiful grain surrounding you, singing with the spirit of the land? You can hear the ancient myths being told on the wind as it brushes the grasses. These lands are part of the origin of that cycle.

But back home it's a whole other beast. There are different seasons, different climate cycles, different land spirits—patterns unique unto themselves. That means that parts of the Wheel of the Year's cycle just don't match up to the heartbeat of where I live. Even the places I have lived that are closer to the climate of England or resembled the landscape are still very different in how they feel and follow the seasons. True, you could squint your eyes on a summer day and a farm in southern New Jersey might pass for the English countryside. But the history, the land, the surrounding waters and creatures all have a different story to tell—worthy of celebration in their own right.

Which is why I feel Lughnasadh is a great reminder that if we are going to observe a Wheel of the Year in our practice, it should make sense with where and when we are living. Lughnasadh is often considered a bit of the oddball sabbat—many folks don't know what to make of it. The solstices and equinoxes have their logical place for sure and are easily understood. When it comes to the cross-quarter days, Beltane and Samhain are well-known and also well-loved, sort of like the "big" holidays of Christmas and Easter in Christianity. Imbolc has a beloved goddess (Brigid) associated with it for many to connect with—along with the human need to feel like we are finally making way against the cold and the dark. At the tail end of winter, we need little excuse to light up some candles and celebrate to get us through to spring. But Lammas (Loaf Mass)? The one I like to call "the bread holiday"? It's usually the one folks most often cite that makes them feel meh or bad about not "feeling" their practice.

Why is that? What is this sabbat all about? Lughnasadh marks the beginning of the harvest season in the Celtic world and is named after the god Lugh. It is celebrated with feasting, games, the making of corn dollies, and special breads that may be ritually sacrificed. It is also a favored day for handfastings in some traditions. According to folklore, Lugh's mother Tailtiu passed away from exhaustion after clearing the land to make way for agriculture. So he held a funeral feast and games to celebrate her memory. Yet the modern observation of this event tends to focus more on him and his deeds than her sacrifice, so that particular detail tends to get a bit lost. The deeper symbolism is that Lughnasadh is a celebration of both the labor of the earth itself and those who work with the land to grow food.

So, what if you're not intimately working with Celtic deities but some other pantheon altogether (or maybe none at all)? What if you're not quite a "Green Witch," and you don't find yourself out in the fields or in the garden? Maybe your harvest season started months prior, so this seems an odd time for a "first harvest." Heck, what if you're sensitive or allergic to gluten and just the idea of a bread holiday (or as I like to call it, Glutengala) gives you hives or an upset stomach? Whatever the reason, you might find it really hard to connect to this particular sabbat. Perhaps maybe you're also feeling this way about some of the others too?

I'm here to help you out. First, it's important to recognize that the Wheel of the Year—as modern practitioners know it, with its eight sabbats—is a fairly recent creation dating back to the mid-twentieth century. It pulls upon the history and mythology of the United Kingdom, piecing together different practices over centuries with modern interpretations. Because it's rooted in lore of the region, it definitely makes the most amount of sense there—though not uniformly depending on the region. As we move further away, we see some overlap with other locations and cultures with some of the sabbats, but the seasons, names, and practices start to differ more and more.

What's a Witch to do? We need to foster connections with where we live and let those be our guide to crafting a wheel that works for our practice. It takes a bit more work, since you'll be creating your own framework, but the results are worth it. Another thing to consider is that we also have a tendency to fixate on days and specific dates. In nature, seasons rarely align perfectly with the calendar, and they can vary in number and length depending on where you live. Instead, consider that the wheel is more about the flow of seasons, not specific days. A Wheel of the Year largely acknowledges the solar cycle—the way the planet reacts as we orbit around the sun, heating up and cooling down as we turn on our axis, affecting each hemisphere and altitude differently. That means while Arizona is experiencing monsoon season, fires are burning in nearby California, and hurricanes and typhoons take up residence in the Atlantic and Pacific oceans—all at once!

Now, I'm not saying to abandon celebrating sabbats on certain days. Having predetermined days is crucial when you're organizing groups, covens, and festivals. Everyone needs to know when and where to meet. But in your personal practice, you can expand past a single-day observance or one official ritual and open yourself up to more ways to explore a season with your magic.

Finding Meaning

Here are some guidelines to help you find more meaning in the sabbats—whether you plan to work with the classic model of the Wheel of the Year or would like to assemble one unique to your practice.

Connect with the Spirit of Place

Where we live is the root of our practice. Yes, we are influenced by our ancestral practices, where we grew up (if it's different than where we are now), the traditions we may initiate into, etc., but there's no denying that ignoring where you reside in your practice is like a fish swimming in air: it doesn't work for long. We are embodied spiritual beings existing in a physical realm, and there's immediate magic to be found right underneath your feet. Tapping into it is a conduit to those distant places—the planet is all interconnected. Trying to connect to a faraway place while being disconnected to where you are makes the process that much harder. It is possible to honor both lands afar (be it your ancestry or tradition's roots) and where you reside. It may require two different kinds of ritual (one from a tradition and one you create to acknowledge the land), but understand that ritual doesn't have to be elaborate. Sometimes even the simplest of gestures can be incredibly powerful.

To help you connect with where you live, look to the folklore of the area. Head over to the anthropology section of the library to dive deeper for starters. What are the stories and history of the place? Who was there before you? What are the landmarks and features of the land? Consider the best way to formally introduce yourself and interact with the land through ritual.

Connect with the Spirit of the Season

Remember that seasons are not run by dates on the calendar. Spring can arrive early, winter can start late. When we start to become more in tune with the goings-on of the weather, we pick up on nature's patterns much more easily. What is the nature of your land's season at this time of year? What are the plants and animals doing? How does the air make you feel? Is there a specific crop or other seasonal event that coincides with this time of year? Is it something you can see being integrated into your personal practice? It doesn't all have to be combined into one ritual, but rather can progress through the whole season, focusing on different characteristics that define the season.

Integrating Deities and Other Practices

As I mentioned earlier, most folks seem to be able to connect with the equinoxes and solstices, and usually some variation of Beltane and Samhain—largely because they can be viewed with a context that fits other cultures, even if the names aren't the same. If you work with deities, spirits, and ancestors that aren't associated with the modern Wheel of the Year, you might find there are myths and practices that do overlap with existing dates—if you wish to celebrate on the same pattern of the wheel. Or you may choose to alter the structure of the wheel to incorporate events that are more relevant to your practice. Is there a festival honoring a certain deity that is special to you? Is there a similar sabbat, but it happens at a slightly different time of year? What has the most amount of meaning for you and your practice?

Simply Honor Life

If you don't work with deities, then consider what this time of year means for you personally. Is there a shift in how you function as the light decreases? Do you transition from vacation to work or school? At the very least, the time of Lugnasadh is about relishing the last days of summer while we're still embedded within them.

Remember Why We Celebrate

Lastly, it's important to consider that ritual is about connection and marking transitions. If you choose to celebrate a sabbat, don't do it just because you feel obligated. Ritual celebrates life itself: the patterns that connect us to nature, to our ancestors, to our communities, and to ourselves. We do it to honor the past, to recognize the cycles of death and life happening around us, and to weave our threads in the larger tapestry of the universe.

Conclusion

I hope these points help inspire you to connect more deeply with where you live and in turn build and strengthen your practice. Also remember, like the seasons, we are ever-changing, so don't be afraid to experiment. You can use established concepts as a foundation to see how they work, then build out from there. Give more traditional approaches a try, but don't be afraid to use what else inspires you, especially if you feel it in your gut. Discover what works best to create the most effective and authentic practice. It may not be what everyone else is doing, but it's your road to walk. Blessings on your path, wherever it leads you!

Cosmic Sway

Robin Ivy Payton

WITH AUGUST COMES FRUITS of spring and summer's efforts. On the farm and in the garden, some gather to harvest berries, corn, and other gifts of the earth. Also known as Lammas in some traditions, this festival of the loaf included baking and blessing bread from the season's first grains. Assembling around food continues to be a primary way we socialize in present time, and in early August locally grown foods are enjoyed and plentiful at farmer's markets, local grocers, and eateries that provide farm to table delights.

Lughnasadh: Time of the Sun King

The felt sense of Lughnasadh celebration is expressed and embedded in its name. *Lugh*, "shine," and *nasad*, "assembly," suggest gathering in the bright Sun during the midpoint of summer. Derived from the Celtic mythology of Lugh, a Sun god, this festival marks the cross quarter, which actually occurs days after the traditional calendar date, August 1. On August 7 or 8, the Sun reaches 15 degrees of the astrology sign Leo, and we are halfway between Summer Solstice and autumnal equinox.

Lughnasadh is a time of shift for the Sun, and waning hours of daylight become more obvious. This time is often chosen for vacations, reunions, outdoor art fairs, concerts, and other events that lend well to clear skies, warm sunshine, and colorful sunsets. A desire to prolong summer enjoyment prompts us to assemble, as if to gather summer rays and gifts before darker, cooler days arrive. We bathe in light and water, absorbing the natural shine of middle summer.

Astrology for Lughnasadh 2022

Lughnasadh follows the July 28 New Moon in Leo and precedes Aquarius Full Moon on August 11. The New Moon and Sun harmonize with Jupiter in Aries, fueling courage, initiative, and momentum. Innovative and creative methods are favored. On August 1, earthy, sensual Virgo Moon accompanies the fiery Leo Sun and, likewise, planets dominate earth and fire signs. Uranus and the North Node in Taurus together break long-held paradigms related to money, stability, and growth. Some will experience an undeniable sense of life purpose and remove all obstacles, clearing their paths to follow their calling. Conventional is replaced by ingenious and radical as these two forces combine. The Moon is void of course from 6:29 p.m. on August 1 to 12:05 a.m. EDT on August 2. Void of course Moon time lends well to parties and gatherings as it tends to help us relax socially and let tensions go.

As Lughnasadh 2022 passes, the Full Moon alights on August 11 in Aquarius, a sign of friendship, community, and collective energy. The Moon approaches Saturn, planet of karma, commitment, and consequence, presenting opportunities to resolve past injustices and to fully engage in devotion to others and our planet. At this time, Mercury, Venus, and Mars, the closest planets to Earth, move forward at their usual pace while some of the more distant planets are retrograde. Having the closer planets direct may be helpful for early August pursuits and plans.

Celebrating Love

Lughnasadh is a traditional time for weddings. One tale in Celtic lore says the Sun God, Lugh, wed Mother Earth on this day. Along with "shine," another root meaning of Lugh is "oath." Vows taken for life, or for one year and a day, feature Venus in either Cancer or Leo this August. For the first ten days, Venus in Cancer blesses home and family and honors the soul journey. Partners wedded now will thrive with emotional intimacy and strong roots. They kindle romance throughout their relationship and are known for unconditional love. Venus crosses the threshold from Cancer to Leo on August 11 at 2:30 p.m. EDT, and tours Leo through early September. Venus in Leo marriages flourish with social friendships, adventures, and unwavering loyalty. The Sun will be in Leo for the entire period of Lughnasadh. This Sun sign radiates a sense of playfulness, longevity, creativity, and joy for partners married from July 22 through August 22, with either Venus sign. Leo rules the heart and spine for love and courage required in enduring relationships. Attune to the felt sense of your own heart at Lughnasadh as the Wheel of the Year turns.

Aligning with Lughnasadh

Create sacred space with colors, crystals, amulets, and any other items needed for your own Lughnasadh rituals. It is traditional for altars to face west, recognizing the waning sun and sunset. Also call your attention to the south, the direction of summer season and the astrological element of fire during Leo time. Invoke the flora and fauna of the south and west. Honor the creatures associated with summer and the south, such as orioles, yellow finches, and blackbirds, whose cycle of power is now. Cougar, Dolphin, Dragonfly, and Lizard also speak from the south and are at the height of their power. Most importantly, call upon beings that hold special meaning for you. Ask for their energy, gifts, and blessings.

The plant world offers magic, abundance, and beauty. Experiencing full blooms now, remember the seeds of their origin, recognizing the passage of time and the Sun's journey. Adorn your space or altar with sunflowers if they're locally in season. Other flowers of yellow, gold, and orange can be planted or harvested as cut flowers.

These same colors may be reflected throughout your home, with clothes, bedding, candles, or even glasses and dinnerware used during high summer. Refresh your kitchen as sacred space for baking with corn and other grains of this harvest sabbat. Corn, grains, fire, and earth inspire the colors of the season, and while orange and golds are more obvious, balance them with the greens and browns of Mother Earth.

Crystals of the same shades can be added to your altar or worn as jewelry. Citrine, yellow agate, and tiger's-eye represent the solar plexus, the body's center of fire. Consider using tiger's-eye, a stone of courage in deep browns imbued with red or gold, for the spirit of the Sun and Leo season. Green crystals such as aventurine and malachite align with the heart center, ruled by the sign of the lion. While aventurine soothes the heart and balances emotional processes, malachite absorbs negativity, supports transformation, and grounds in personal growth.

Meditating on the tarot can be helpful at this cross-quarter time. Fan out your cards and select some wands (also called rods) and pentacles that draw your attention. Open your intuition beyond thinking to perceiving, and simply listen through your third eye and heart. In the tarot, pentacles symbolize earth, our harvest, and wands are the symbol of fire.

At Lughnasadh, Leo Sun rules creative force, which can be channeled into crafts and projects. Design a wand from a tree branch and add summer crystals or shells. This is a traditional time to create a besom, the broom used to clear sacred space. The broom handle symbolizes wands, the fire element, while the brush is from fibers of the earth. Seek instructions online or do it yourself with original ideas and materials. The besom can be used year-round to cleanse your space symbolically or physically. Hang it on a door for protection or display it in the kitchen as assurance that the Sun and summer's harvest will once again return.

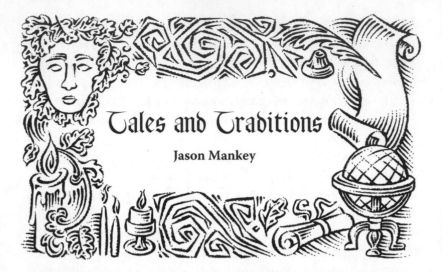

Tales and Traditions

Jason Mankey

TRADITIONALLY LAMMAS (OR LUGHNASSA) is a celebration of the grain harvest. In Ireland and other parts of the British Isles the first harvest of the year was in early August and generally for cereal crops such as wheat, barley, and oats. An alternative name for Lammas is "First Fruits," an apt description for the first of the three major harvest festivals on the Wheel of the Year (the other two being Mabon and Samhain of course). While I have never lived in an area where the grain harvest was brought in during the first week of August, I still enjoy celebrating both bread and cereal crops at Lammas, and generally do so by honoring various goddesses of the grain.

Lammas: Goddesses of the Grain

The most famous grain goddess is the Greek deity Demeter. Demeter is the sister of Zeus and one of the twelve (or thirteen) Olympians who hold court upon Mount Olympus. Unlike many of the other Olympians, Demeter is intimately involved with the mortal world. It's her very presence that makes the earth fertile and provides for the harvest.

But traditionally Demeter is more than just a fertility goddess and the lady of the corn, her influence spreads into nearly every facet of our lives. Agriculture has long been hailed as a civilizing force; large-scale farming requires cooperation and a variety of people undertaking different sorts of labor, making Demeter a goddess of civilization. Because large societies require at least a few rules, Demeter is also a goddess of law, order, and justice.

Demeter is often pictured with her daughter Persephone (or Kore), and together the two goddesses symbolize the grain harvest. In the most well-known tale of Demeter and Persephone, Persephone is abducted by Hades, the god of the underworld. Demeter goes into mourning and the earth's fertility ceases. Eventually Demeter is reunited with her daughter, but for only a portion of the year. When Persephone returns to the underworld, the earth goes fallow as Demeter mourns, and when Persephone returns in the spring, Demeter once more gives her gifts of fertility and abundance.

There are deeper meanings in the pairing of Demeter and Persephone than their most popular myths suggest. Just as Persephone goes into the underworld, the roots of the grain also reach underground. The first grain harvest is generally joyous, but side by side with that joy is death. There is no flour without the death of the wheat, and the crops cannot return again in the spring without the fertility of the soil brought about by decay, rot, and death.

The celebration of the cycle of death and rebirth involving Demeter and Persephone reached its height at Eleusis, a religious site about half a day's walk from the Greek city of Athens. At the Eleusian Mysteries worshippers mourned with Demeter as she lost her daughter but took solace in the idea that all which dies is born again. The mysteries of Eleusis promised hope in the afterlife and lasted in ancient Greece (and later the Roman Empire) for a few thousand years. The very word "mystery" comes from the Greek word *mysterion*, which means a secret rite. Every time we honor Demeter and her daughter, we tap into the energy of her mysteries.

In many communities throughout Ireland, Scotland, and England the grain harvest was symbolized by a female figure made from grain sheaves. Today this figure is most commonly known as the *Cailleach*. Depending on where one lived (traditions varied from village to village), the Cailleach was either seen as a beneficial or menacing figure. If her reputation was positive, she was often given a seat of honor at harvest feasts. If it was negative, she was generally set apart from the proceedings and used as a figure to scare children (Hutton 1996, 337–338).

The varying interpretations for the Cailleach most likely have to do with how the harvest was perceived among various communities. For some people the harvest was a time for unbridled joy—the hard work was done and there was most likely plenty (at least for a time). For others, the harvest was the "beginning of the end," and they saw it as symbolizing the coming winter. Many Witches honor the Cailleach as a Crone goddess, seeing within her not just the bounty of the harvest, but the intelligence and wisdom needed to take the crops in.

Isis was the goddess of just about everything in the ancient world, and that includes the grain harvest. She was intimately associated with both the river Nile and the fertile soil around it. According to some versions of her myth, it was the tears of Isis that filled the Nile, allowing the ancient Egyptians to partake in the harvest. In other versions, it was her lover, Osiris, who was seen as the waters, while she was the earth. When the Nile overflowed its banks, it was seen as the union of the two deities, a union the crops of Egypt depended upon.

Nissaba (sometimes spelled Nisaba) was one of several Sumerian grain goddesses, but her dominion extended far past ancient Sumer's barley fields. Nissaba was the goddess of all of Sumer's grasses, including the reeds which were used to write upon Sumer's cuneiform tablets. Because of her association with scribes and writing, Nissaba was revered as a goddess of wisdom and learning. As most early Sumerian records were used to keep track of agricultural goods, Nissaba was also a goddess of mathematics, commerce, and accounting.

Asherah was a major Canaanite goddess and was also once worshipped among the Hebrews of Israel (and was possibly even married to the god Yahweh). While Yahweh was worshipped in his large temple in Jerusalem, Asherah tended to be honored among the common folk who would often worship her under a simple wooden pole. To honor Asherah, cakes would be baked in her shape and honor, marking her as a goddess of the grain and the harvest.

If you choose to honor a grain and harvest goddess at Lammas, be sure to thank them for the gifts of the season by name, and to leave them a gift of some sort. Libations of bread, beer, or anything else made from the gifts of the earth are especially appropriate. And don't forget to invite whatever goddess you invoke to partake in any harvest feasting you might do.

References

Burkert, Walter. *Greek Religion.* Cambridge MA: Harvard University Press, 1985.

Farrar, Janet, and Stewart Farrar. *The Witches' Goddess: The Feminine Principle of Divinity.* Custer, WA: Phoenix Publishing, 1987.

Hutton, Ronald. *The Stations of the Sun: A History of the Ritual Year in Britain.* Oxford: Oxford University Press, 1996.

Mankey, Jason. *Witch's Wheel of the Year: Rituals for Circles, Solitaries & Covens.* Woodbury, MN: Llewellyn Publications, 2019.

Feasts and Treats

Elizabeth Barrette

LAMMAS IS THE FESTIVAL of grain. At this time, the earliest ripening grains are harvested, but for others the harvest still remains uncertain. Wheat and buckwheat are among the traditional grains of Europe, while quinoa comes from South America. The god goes into the grain and dies to be reborn as the year wheel turns.

Grateful Grain Burgers

Veggie burgers come in many styles. While there are now many artificial meat products, all of them are ultra-processed products. Whole plant foods offer healthier choices and delicious flavors. This version uses a combination of black beans, mushrooms, and grains so the patties hold together well in cooking.

Prep time: 45 minutes

Cooking time: 8 minutes roasting, plus 6–8 minutes frying or 15–20 minutes baking

Servings: 6–8

1 tablespoon flaxseed meal
3 tablespoons water
olive oil cooking spray
1 can (15 ounces) of black beans

8 ounces portabella mushrooms
1 carrot (about ⅜ cup shredded)
1 clove of garlic
¼ teaspoon Hawaiian red salt
¼ teaspoon black pepper
¼ teaspoon chipotle pepper
½ cup cooked quinoa
¼ cup cooked wheat berries
¼ cup cooked buckwheat groats
2 tablespoons minced creamed coconut
2 beefsteak tomatoes
1 sweet onion
whole-grain buns
cheese slices or spreadable vegan cheese
alfalfa sprouts

Prepare for cooking the Grateful Grain Burgers with the method of your choice. They can be grilled, baked, or fried.

Preheat an oven to 400°F. Line two baking sheets with aluminum foil and spray with olive oil. (If you don't have it as cooking spray, pour a little olive oil on each sheet and brush it around.)

Make a "flax egg." Measure 1 tablespoon flaxseed meal and 3 tablespoons water into a small bowl. Whisk to combine. Set aside for 10 minutes to thicken. (This vegan substitute behaves like an egg in most recipes.)

Open the can of black beans and pour off the liquid. Rinse the black beans and put them in a colander to drain.

Rinse the portabella mushrooms. (Keep the gill side down to avoid getting soggy. Water will run off the top of the cap.) Dice them into small pieces, then spread them on a baking sheet.

Divide the black beans in half. Spread one half of them on a baking sheet. Put the other half in a small mixing bowl.

Roast the mushrooms and the black beans at 400°F for about 8 minutes. The beans should dry out and start to split. The mushrooms should sweat and start to soften. Then drain the mushrooms.

Let them and the beans cool somewhat before adding them to the other ingredients.

While the vegetables are roasting, rinse and shred the carrot. You can also use frozen spiralized carrot, in which case simply smack the bag against the counter to shatter the spirals into small fragments. You need about ⅜ cup of shreds. Add the carrot shreds to the black beans in the mixing bowl.

Peel and mince 1 clove of garlic. Add it to the mixing bowl.

Add ¼ teaspoon Hawaiian red salt, ¼ teaspoon black pepper, and ¼ teaspoon chipotle pepper to the mixing bowl. Pour the flax egg into the mixing bowl. Mash everything together to form a thick paste.

In a large mixing bowl, combine ½ cup cooked quinoa, ¼ cup cooked wheat berries, and ¼ cup cooked buckwheat groats. Add the whole roasted black beans and the chopped mushrooms. Stir together.

Creamed coconut should be solid at room temperature; if not, you can chill it in the refrigerator. Mince the creamed coconut until you have 2 tablespoons of small crumbles. It should look a lot like minced suet and will behave the same in the recipe, melting like the beef fat in a hamburger. Stir the minced creamed coconut into the large mixing bowl.

Add the mashed black beans to the large mixing bowl. Fold and stir until everything is well combined. You should have a stiff dough with visible chunks in it that sticks together well. If the dough is too crumbly, add more of a wet ingredient such as another flax egg. If it is too runny, add more of a dry ingredient such as cooked wheat berries.

Shape the dough into palm-size patties and cook them. (This recipe makes 6–8 patties.) For grilling or frying, cook the Grateful Grain Burgers 3–4 minutes per side, flipping carefully. For baking, heat the oven to 350°F and cook the patties until heated through, about 15–20 minutes.

Slice two beefsteak tomatoes. (Use an heirloom variety for more flavor if possible.) Slice a sweet onion.

Place each patty on a whole-grain bun and top it with a slice of cheese (or a spoonful of vegan spreadable cheese), a slice of beef-steak tomato, a slice of sweet onion, and alfalfa sprouts.

Summer Vegetable Medley

This recipe relies on summer vegetables in their peak season, so use whatever's fresh in your area. The rainbow of colors symbolize the mingled energies of the sun and the earth. Honey brings the industrious energy of bees.

Prep time: 30 minutes
Cooking time: 5–10
Servings: 5–7

1 small zucchini
1 small yellow squash (summer or patty pan)
1 medium purple eggplant
1 red bell pepper
1 orange bell pepper
1 green bell pepper
1 sweet onion
1 tablespoon fresh grated ginger
1 tablespoon honey
zest and juice of 1 lemon
¼ cup minced fresh basil
¼ cup minced fresh marjoram
2 tablespoons ghee (clarified butter)

Rinse the zucchini, yellow squash, and eggplant. Remove the ends, then chop the flesh into bite-sized chunks. Place in a mixing bowl.

Rinse the bell peppers and cut them into strips. Add to the mixing bowl.

Peel the sweet onion and chop it into bite-sized chunks. Add to the mixing bowl.

In a small bowl, combine 1 tablespoon fresh grated ginger, 1 tablespoon honey, and the zest and juice of 1 lemon.

Add ¼ cup minced fresh basil and ¼ cup minced fresh marjoram to the vegetables, then toss gently to combine.

Put a skillet on medium heat and melt 2 tablespoons ghee. Add the vegetables and cook, stirring constantly, until they soften (about 5–10 minutes).

Grilled Peaches

Peaches are the star fruit of late summer. Their dripping sweetness brings joy, and the round yellow shape stands for the sun. The lemon, ginger, and honey flavors match well with the same set from the Summer Vegetable Medley.

Prep time: 10 minutes
Cookie time: 10–12
Servings: 6

½ cup lemon juice
¼ cup honey
1 tablespoon fresh grated ginger
¼ teaspoon salt
6 freestone peaches, halved and pitted
lemon sorbet (optional)

In a small bowl, stir together ½ cup lemon juice, ¼ cup honey, 1 tablespoon fresh grated ginger, and ¼ teaspoon salt.

Peel the peaches, cut them in half, and pop out the pits. Put the peach halves into a plastic zip bag. Pour in the marinade and seal the bag. Tilt the bag to coat the peaches completely. Refrigerate for 20 minutes.

Remove the peaches from the bag. Grill the peach halves until caramelized and tender, about 5–6 minutes per side. Serve hot with optional lemon sorbet.

Crafty Crafts

Charlie Rainbow Wolf

LAMMAS—ALSO CALLED LUGHNASSADH or Lugnasad—marks the harvesting of the first grain and honors the god Lugh. The word Lammas comes from the Old English *hlafmæsse*, which means "loaf mass." It shows just how important the grain harvest was.

This is the time of year when the grain mother is ripe, when she blesses us with her bounty, and when there's a flurry of activity to start gathering in the yield for the rapidly approaching winter. In his role as John Barleycorn, Lugh must sacrifice himself so that others might be fed. He is both the seed that returns to the earth in spring to provide the next crop and the grain that is turned into flour to feed and sustain his children over the winter.

Bread Dough Ornaments

Here at The Keep, we mark this grain festival by baking bread and starting an ale to enjoy at the winter solstice. It's a good time for making bread dough ornaments to later be thrown in the fire at Samhain or hung on the tree at Yule. This is a different recipe than bread you eat. Preserve them well and they will last for several seasons.

Materials

Flour: Cheap all-purpose flour is appropriate; at least a pound is
    needed.

Salt: Salt is an excellent preservative. Use everyday table salt. 1 cup
    salt to 4 cups flour is required, so get a lot!

Water: Tap water is good.

Mixing bowl and spoon

Rolling pin

Toothpick or straw or old knitting needle

Cookie sheets and parchment paper

Cutters and textures: Use what's on hand; because the items are
    food safe (though not particularly tasty), existing cookware is
    fine.

Decorations: Paint and brushes, glitter, glue, ribbon; let your imagination go!

Sealant: I use a clear polyurethane spray, but a "paint" made of thinned craft glue will also work—Mod Podge is possibly the best option.

Cost: This goes from pennies upward. At time of writing, a 10-pound bag of flour was less than $3 and a 2-pound box of salt around the same. Decorations can be spendy or, again, scavenge what you already have. Mod Podge is $10 for a 1-pound tub. Polyurethane spray sealant is $5 and up.

Time spent: An afternoon, plus drying time.

Mix It Up!

The recipe is easy: 4 cups flour, 1 cup salt, and water to mix. The dough needs to be stiff, like Play-Doh or pastry; it has to hold its shape. Sprinkle some flour onto the countertop or table and roll the dough out with the rolling pin. Add texture if desired, and cut the dough into shapes. The dough can also be used to build something rather than cutting it out; a small plaited loaf, a green man—or if these are being made to use at Yule, think about making snowflakes and snowmen. Use a toothpick, drinking straw, or an old knitting needle to cut a hole for hanging the ornament, if desired.

Line a cookie sheet with parchment paper and place the dough onto it. Bake them in a 300°F oven for approximately an hour. The time depends on the thickness of the dough; they need to be hard and solid but not burned. (Although the burned ones can always just be painted; I won't tell).

Once the dough is cooled, it's time to decorate. How this is done is a personal choice; no two ornaments are ever exactly the same. Once they are embellished and thoroughly dry, apply a generous sealant using either the Mod Podge or the polyurethane spray. (Spraying is best done outside, so there's less mess and smell in the work area.) Add ribbon or another hanger (if applicable) to complete the salt dough ornament.

This is a fun group activity but it is just as enjoyable if you're on your own. Kids particularly love getting messy with the dough and the decorations. You might even start an annual tradition!

References

Christmas Doughcrafts by Lorraine Bodger, 1986.

Creative Doughcrafts by Patricia Hughes, 1999.

55 Celebration Doughcraft Designs by Linda Rogers, 1996.

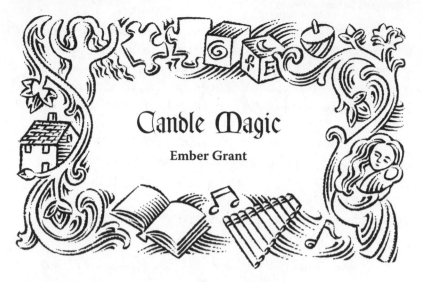

Candle Magic

Ember Grant

LUGH, THE MANY-SKILLED, is a significant figure in Celtic cultures. Lughnasadh means "the assembly of Lugh." This time of year around August 1 has long been a time to celebrate this hero. In addition, the first harvest typically occurs around this time.

Burning Spell for Letting Go

Lughnasadh is an ideal sabbat for letting go of things you no longer need. It's also a good time to examine your life to see if anything is holding you back or keeping you from reaching your potential. Agriculturally, at this time of year we celebrate the "first harvest" but, often, to make room for the good things in your life, you must clear away what's no longer needed. Think of it this way—burning the field, so to speak, not only clears the area but can regenerate the land and nourish it for new growth.

Fire is a fierce element and, like all the elements, it can be destructive yet transformative as a result. Because of its ability to "burn through" barriers to success, the element of fire is useful for spells that help you make progress, clear obstacles, and make necessary changes in your life.

You will need one candle and a section of ribbon or twine approximately 6 inches long. Try to find a black candle for this spell, or use white. You'll also need a piece of ribbon or twine (any color) to represent your obstacle or challenge. The ribbon needs to be long enough for you to hold safely over the candle flame without burning your fingers.

Prepare the candle and your sacred space as desired. Light the candle. Hold the ribbon and visualize it as a barrier you need to get through. It can be a fear, bad habit, or anything you're trying to overcome. It can even be a relationship that is holding you back or anything you feel is a weight that's holding you down. Name it out loud as you hold the ribbon:

This ribbon represents (what you're trying to break free from).

Hold the ribbon horizontally in the candle flame as you visualize overcoming your barrier. When it's burned in half, say:

Barrier removed, complication severed, no obstacle resists, I am no longer tethered.

Bury the pieces of ribbon in separate places or throw them into separate waste receptacles. Allow the candle to burn out. You can relight it over several days, if necessary. In fact, to increase the potency of this spell, repeat it every day for ten days.

"Good Morning" Candle Spell

We often associate candles with evening and nighttime rituals, but this spell is intended for the morning. It's a "good start" spell for the day, especially on days when you can use a boost of positive energy.

Mornings, with the sunrise, are often viewed as a "fresh" or "new" start—each day a chance to start over. We say phrases like "Things will look better in the morning" or "You'll gain a new perspective in the light of day." There is much folklore about daybreak and the sun, with the new dawn's ability to dispel evil, which can't abide the light. And, of course, the myths of many cultures involve worship of the sun or a solar deity; in fact, the Celtic hero-god Lugh (for whom this sabbat is named) was associated with the sun.

If possible, burn the candle as you prepare for your day—while getting dressed, enjoying your morning coffee or tea, eating breakfast, or even while exercising. You can burn it while you're in the shower or watering the plants—just make sure you don't wander too far from the candle while it's burning.

A white candle is a good, all-purpose choice, but yellow or gold are appropriate as well; you can use any color that makes you happy. That's the point, really—to brighten your day both literally and figuratively. Burn the candle in whatever holder suits the candle you've chosen. If possible, choose a candle or holder adorned with sun shapes, engrave sun symbols on the candle, or both.

Visualize the sun's power as represented by the burning candle; both are essential for life. Obviously the sun helps make life possible, but fire, too, is essential—think of all the advancements in human civilization that have been accomplished because humans learned how to use fire. As with the sun, many cultures have myths about how humanity came to possess the gift of fire. These two precious sources of light and heat are truly life-giving. Symbolically, happy people are said to have a "sunny" disposition, energetic people are said to possess a "spark," and intelligent people are "bright" or "brilliant."

Since you may not have time to let the candle burn out completely, you can snuff it out and relight it whenever you need it. You can keep this candle on your table, dresser, even the bathroom counter. Let it be a symbol and reminder of a bright day ahead. If necessary, focus on anything specific you anticipate for the day ahead that may cause difficulty. You can also use the candle to promote general positive energy and protection.

Each time you light it, say these words:

Fire light my way today, fierce and bright throughout the day;
my inner flame keeps harm at bay, no matter what may come
my way.

Light the Way

In Celtic myth, there was a prophecy that Lugh would kill his grandfather. To try and avoid his fate, the grandfather locked Lugh and his mother in a box and tossed them into the sea. Of course, they were rescued and Lugh became a great hero. The motif of a child foretold to overthrow a parent or grandparent is common in mythology.

Use this candle spell to guide the way for anyone who is "lost"— either literally or metaphorically. Or, use it for yourself. Remember, if you're performing the spell for another person, get their consent if possible. This spell can also be used for a pet or even an object.

You will need three yellow candles of any size. Arrange them in appropriate containers or on a large plate. Visualize your need and the outcome. As you light each candle, whisper these words:

In sky or sea or ground,
let what is lost be found.
I ask the aid of Lugh
to find the path that's true.

Allow the candles to burn out and discard them.

Lammas Ritual

Laura Tempest Zakroff

WHEN FOLKS TALK ABOUT celebrating a good harvest, we are often thinking about what we're receiving from that harvest: fruits, vegetables, grains, and other food to get us through the winter. We may also be remembering the months of our own labor of tending to the land. All those hours watering, weeding, tending, and protecting our crops has paid off. We may also offer thanks to a particular deity for blessing our harvest.

As I look out at my yard and around my neighborhood in the late summer, I see plants that are starting to show the wear of producing and the effects of long exposure to sun and thunderstorms. There's a sense of urgency to get those last flowers out and bear that fruit before the first kiss of autumn arrives. The land itself feels tired but persistent and determined. It has put in as much labor as we have, working alongside and with us to nurture our gardens.

Giving Back Gratitude

It's good to celebrate the harvest, but it's just as important to honor our relationship with the land as well. Consider what we can give back to it in appreciation for its efforts. This act of giving back can not only strengthen our bond with the land, it can also provide physical and metaphysical sustenance for the year to come.

It's very easy to give back to the land and show it some gratitude beyond the daily maintenance. Just taking a little time out of your day to collect an offering, present it to the land, and show it some respect can make a big difference. You can do it just once on a specific day or offer several kinds of offerings over the course of a week, month, or season. My favorite time to make an offering is early morning or at sunset—those liminal times where the world around us is transitioning. I do them as I feel inspired by the land.

Offerings

Here are just a few ideas of different kinds of offerings you can make for the land:

• Compost replenishes the nutrients in the soil. I keep a small compost can in my kitchen to collect eggshells, coffee grounds, peels, and other greens. Then I deposit those in my larger bin outside and distribute the compost when it's ready. Easy to do if you have a yard and the space to work with, but not ideal for apartments, small spaces, and city-living, though many cities now offer compost pick-up as well, so you can contribute that way if your city participates.

• Water is a precious resource, so even though it seems ordinary, to offer water to the land still has a lot of power. Be careful not to overwater, pay attention to the needs of the land.

• Milk and honey are traditional and very effective. Be careful how and where you leave these gifts so as not to attract unwanted pests. You might want to have consecrated bowls or plates just for this task that you can tend to regularly.

• Offerings from the harvest. Many gardeners I know always leave a portion of their harvest for the land and the wildlife to enjoy. If you didn't grow the food yourself but got it from a local farmstand or market, then you can make an offering from that instead.

• Performing dance, poetry, or song for the land is perfect for creative folks; our own talents are beautiful gifts that give nourishing energy to the land. You can incorporate these into a larger ritual as well.

• Biodegradable art. I love to make dolls from what's in my garden, collecting sticks, big leaves, seed pods, and flowers to make a simple doll that I leave in certain spots of the yard that feel right. You can also gather bouquets locally and make offerings of them.

• Plant indigenous and native plants. Making the effort to work with plants that are native to the land when possible often helps bring balance to the garden.

• Giving of our own bodies—saliva, hair, breath, blood—is not only a powerful way to connect with the land, but also can add back vital nutrients to the earth. (If your hair is chemically treated, I'd skip this one.) Also, I suggest burying blood versus leaving it on the surface. Taking time to talk with the land is a gift of breath.

• Locally produced beverages: tea, wine, beer, cider, mead, etc. If you make your own spirits or support a local business that does, this is another traditional offering that tends to be well received by the land spirits. Tea is perfect if you don't want to use an alcoholic beverage.

• Cleaning up and clearing trash and debris, or removing invasive plants, etc. can show deep appreciation for the land. Be sure not to disturb habitats and ecosystems though—keep some areas of fallen leaves for insects and other animals to weather the winter in.

• Beautifying the landscape with sustainable art and sculpture. Adding a bird fountain and a pond to our yard created new habitats and opportunities for the wildlife in our area. Rocks, ceramics, and concrete sculptures can also do the same while beautifying the space.

• Donate to local organizations. Short on time, don't have the space to grow things, or a good spot where you can leave offerings? Consider donating (if you have money) or volunteering (if you have time) to local groups who work with the land. Near where I live, there is a city-farm program that helps inner-city children learn about nature and how to grow sustainably. There is also a weekly summer plant meetup that raises money for charity while sharing plant wisdom. Just a quick online search should yield several options for nearly any area, or you can donate to a favorite sacred site, even if it's not local.

Conclusion

You don't have to come up with elaborate or complex rituals to do any of these things. Sometimes the most simple and unassuming gestures can be the most profound and powerful. Follow your intuition, be emotionally open to the land as you make your offering, and give yourself some time to listen in return. A few quiet moments of reflection can yield a definitive response or bestow wisdom to help foster the relationship further.

If you feel you must say something as you make your offering, here is a simple rhyme:

> *To the keepers of the land, spirits of earth*
> *Please accept this offering that I give forth.*

Notes

Notes

Notes

Notes

Mabon

Nature's Sleep: The Importance of Dormancy

Kate Freuler

MABON, OR THE AUTUMN equinox, is the date when day and night are of equal length. In the northern hemisphere, this marks the beginning of the dark season when much of nature falls into a dormant state. The equinox heralds the withering of leaves, the shrivelling of the last flowers, and the collection of the final harvests. The earth becomes barren and dark as the remnants of summer are laid to rest. Sometimes autumn can feel melancholy, like endings and death surround us as we say goodbye to the sun, but it's important to notice the beauty and purpose of this part of the great cycle.

Dormancy is often confused with death—many times you'll hear people say that trees and plants "die" in fall—but the state of dormancy is better compared to sleep. It's a restorative time for the earth, a period of hidden growth, repose, regeneration, cleansing, and deep inner renewal. The earth's cycles are reflected in our life experiences, including periods of dormancy. We ourselves are made of the earth, the sky, the rivers, and the air so it only makes sense that we also have the seasons within us. Examining the purpose of darkness and inactivity in nature and all the good it eventually brings forth can help us navigate the empty times of our own existence. These times may not always directly correspond with the earth's seasons, but rather take the form of endings in our inner and outer lives. Some examples are severing relationships, moving homes, switching jobs, going through a phase of introspection, or naturally receding from social doings to think and reflect. These experiences almost always lead to personal growth and positive change just as winter eventually leads to spring.

Spiritual Dormancy

A dormant phase in life can occur during a waiting period in between projects, when dealing with change or loss, or while doing shadow work. Shadow work is the act of looking inward at ourselves and confronting our deeply ingrained behaviours, feelings, and needs. This can be taxing emotionally and spiritually, which only further proves the importance of rest during transformation. Rest and inactivity are often frowned upon in our society; we're under constant pressure to appear productive, to perform, and to be on the go. When we compare this unrelenting, hyper-industrious mindset to the natural world around us, the stark contrast highlights just how unhealthy and harmful it really is. Around Mabon, animals answer the instinctive call to rest and regenerate by preparing for hibernation, which ensures their future survival. Trees shake their expired leaves off with relief, releasing that which is no longer useful. Plants drop the heavy seed pods they worked so hard to create and recede into themselves for the season. The entire natural world accepts this time of rest in stride. Why is it so hard for people to do the same?

Taking a lesson from the earth by observing seasonal changes around Mabon, we can appreciate our own dormant times for what they are: a chance to build strength, take stock, and repair. It's a time to look gently down inside ourselves and see what needs attention, which is what shadow work is all about. It's a good time to rethink what it means to "rest" and unlearn some toxic beliefs. Reframing the idea of rest means removing its associations with laziness and shame and replacing them with an appreciation for creativity, strength building, and cleansing. It can be tough to recondition our thinking regarding dormancy, but nature makes it clear to us every winter just how important and natural it is.

Growth in the Shadows

While dormant trees and plants may look "dead," they're actually very much alive, their cells conserving energy for future growth. The parts that appear "dead" are simply no longer needed and have served their purpose, so the trees and plants let them go. This shedding action is something we need to do in our own personal lives every so often too; clinging to that which is over, obsolete, or has otherwise served its purpose is an exercise in futility and only holds us back from reaching our potential. Sometimes this is a personal trait that needs to be cast off, and other times it's an outside circumstance or person with whom we need to cut ties.

Dormancy isn't always easy. It can feel like we're just hanging in there conserving energy while the things we've outgrown fall away. At best, this can feel boring, at worst depressing or frightening. To get through change, it's normal to move away from the herd, withdraw socially, and spend more time alone. Many people even naturally sync up with the rhythm of the Wheel of the Year, becoming introspective and isolated as the nights lengthen.

Although it's sometimes unsettling, this experience is also an opportunity to really look inward while nourishing the newest emerging parts of ourselves based on the lessons of the past season.

As the dark season rolls onward, you'll begin to see flashes of hope. You'll notice signs of growth and creation stirring deep within your spirit, giving you glimpses of what's to come and who you are growing into. This is all part of your spiritual development and, in the end, it will make perfect sense.

Let the Seasons Guide You

Nature's relationship with the dark and cold is a metaphor for how shadow work and spiritual dormancy play out within our lives. Here are some of the ways that the dark months interact with the earth and how those interactions can be applied to our personal experiences as we grow and change.

Strength: Wild plants that survive fall and winter dormancy tend to be very strong. This same concept can be applied to our own personal issues. A period of hardship is often necessary in order to reach our full potential. No successful or well-rounded person will tell you that they achieved all their goals easily; there is always failure, doubt, and times of regrouping along the path. After that, they came back stronger and smarter and tried again. This builds resilience, determination, and wisdom. Just as the cold months make for stronger plants, our own periods of dormancy can provide us with the energy and resources to reemerge stronger and more determined than ever.

Productivity: Trees need to have a period of rest, which is brought on by shortened days and low temperatures, in order to build up the energy to grow new leaves. Without the dark months, they wouldn't have a chance to do this and would simply die. If a fruit tree doesn't get a long enough dormant season, it will produce less fruit the following year. The same can be said of you: if you don't get enough rest, you won't be as productive in any area of your life. This can, of course, be seen in terms of getting enough sleep at night (which is also important!) but also in the larger picture of your own achievements. You need time to turn inward, to work on yourself in order to better interact with your outer life. This rest period, while it may feel unproductive, is in fact a wonderful breeding ground of creativity that will result in a flourish of action when the time is right.

Protection: Cold and darkness kill diseases and infestations on plants and trees. This means that dormancy is part of the healing process. You may experience something similar when you enter your state of spiritual dormancy and shed toxic or unnecessary connections to people or things. Letting go of familiar things can be painful, just like the winter's frozen touch, but absolutely necessary. Parasitic relationships and negativity that have been dragging you down can be stamped out during your shadow work, just like when the cold kills mold and pests in a garden.

Cleansing: Snow is useful to the health of ecosystems in many ways. It provides insulation for the earth, much like a warm blanket while nature sleeps. A heavy snowfall will also ensure the replenishment of lakes, streams, and wetlands. When the snow melts away in spring, it takes with it all kinds of debris and waste to allow room for new life. As you rest and withdraw during your soul-winter, you will also experience the very-much-needed cleansing of the things that no longer have a purpose in your life.

A Frost Ritual for Strength

This simple working draws upon the strengthening aspects of the cold. It also helps dismantle the idea that cold, darkness, and death are "bad," focusing instead on the positive aspects of an icy frost. Around Mabon, you may start to notice frost forming on the ground overnight and that the strongest plants survive it. This is a perfect opportunity to identify a project, idea, or quality of yourself you'd like to strengthen and incorporate it into a ritual. Some areas of focus for this working can be your self-confidence, resilience, health, or any aspect of your life that needs reinforcements.

On a night that you know there will be frost, write a word or design a symbol for your concern. Draw the symbol or write the word on a small piece of paper. After dark, place the paper outdoors on the grass. If it's windy, secure it with a stone or heavy object. As you place the paper on the ground, spend a moment visualizing yourself demonstrating the traits you wish to strengthen in perfect confidence. Leave the paper there overnight. First thing in the morning, go retrieve your frosty paper. Take the paper indoors and let the frost melt, imagining the dampness infusing your symbol with strength and resilience. Stash the paper somewhere private for the winter and allow the strength you need to manifest over the dark months of rest.

Growth in Darkness

Mabon marks the beginning of the dormant phase in nature, which mirrors the dark seasons in your own life. The equinox is a liminal time where one thing ends and another begins. Understanding that dormancy is perfectly natural and healthy may help you find peace and rhythm within the cycles of nature and within your spirit. You might even learn to enjoy these quiet times, knowing that they're supporting the wonderful things that are to come from within you.

Cosmic Sway

Robin Ivy Payton

THE SUN SITS DIRECTLY above the earth's equator, darkness and light share equal time, and autumn's coolness rises as summer's warmth lets go. The autumnal equinox arrives with the Sun's move to Libra on September 22 at 9:04 p.m. EDT. The Sabian symbol for the first degree of Libra is a perfectly formed butterfly pinned with a dart. The juxtaposition of life to death and animate to unmoving reflect this moment of transition. The butterfly's beauty and symmetry are the harmony of daylight and nighttime, yin and yang in balance. The dart represents our desire to hold this moment of perfection where we gather apples, squashes, and other fruits of the season and revel in the light, which soon we must let go. Autumn's other name, fall, describes the Sun's journey downward and our own movement inward to a time of recollection.

Autumn Astrology

At this year's autumnal equinox, the Moon wanes toward balsamic with New Moon in Libra on September 25. Mercury retrograde in Libra is heading back to Virgo to station direct on October 2.

Mercury leads personal and business partners to revisit conversations and plans. As Mercury retraces steps into practical and earthy Virgo, we begin to outline actions for the near future while maintaining flexibility through these retrograde days. Free yourself to focus more on process than results. Let go of outdated ideas and ideals to make room for something new. Autumn season and waning Moon signal this as a time for release.

Venus travels Virgo until September 29 and then moves into Libra, the sign of love and the power of two. Mercury retrograde approaches Venus first, and they meet in a Virgo kiss. This conjunction brings minds and hearts together for mutual agreements and vows. Reconnecting, reconciling, and reevaluating happens organically now, or can be sought after from New Moon through September's end. The majority of planets in air and earth signs favor both reimagining and taking steps to rejuvenate and rebuild.

Peaceful Warrior

Libra is also a sign of justice and peace. We meet, merge, and collaborate for harmony and wholeness. Acknowledging opposites and polarities, noticing how one thing dissolves as another arises. Practice equanimity, the ability to stay centered through changing experiences. Like standing half in shadow, half in light, sensing composure and balance as you steady when the Libra scales sway in one direction or another.

The Full Moon in Aries on October 9 is the Hunter Moon, the Moon of the Warrior. While Aries Full Moon means action, initiative, and sometimes confrontation, Venus will be peacefully in Libra, her home sign. Side by side with the Sun, Venus is opposite the Moon, offering temperance and love to Full Moon circumstance and emotions. Between equinox and Full Moon, find the peaceful warrior within, the one who rallies for tranquility and equality.

Astrological Activities

The fall equinox is a time for recollection. As you harvest or enjoy the fruits of the garden and orchards, also gather mementos and memories. Begin a journal of reflections or collect photos from spring and summer festivities. Dry fall flowers for wreaths and arrangements. Align with Libra's sense of clarity by adding clear quartz to an altar or spell. And while the Sun highlights partnership, rose quartz harmonizes relationships and encourages inner contentment.

A detoxifying cleanse pairs well with the seasonal transition. Venus will be in Virgo, sign of health and purification, during the equinox and through September 29. This planetary placement favors healthier habits as well as simple dietary shifts. Venus rules our outward appearance, our skin, and our smile. Detoxify from within by consuming warm water with lemon, decaffeinated herbal teas, and greens like parsley and cruciferous vegetables. As you cleanse and nourish your inner body, your skin may clear and appear more radiant. Intermittent fasting—such as eating all meals within eight hours each day—or replacing your usual diet with kitchari for five to seven days are other ways to calm and restore your digestive system. As always, check with a health professional to see if a cleanse is appropriate for you.

Balance external advice and information with inner wisdom with tarot reading. Gaze into cards like High Priestess and Empress, the maiden and mother whose mythology explains the oncoming winter. Other cards of the season include the Hanged Man who suggests stillness and a balance of darkness and light. Justice and Judgment show the essence of Libra as well. Arrange these intuitively, intuiting what each has to offer your journey at this time.

Face west, connecting to sunset on your evening of choice, invoking the beings or memories associated with this direction. As the sun disappears over the horizon, acknowledge that after an abundant season of activity, rest and release are essential.

As we dance, then we dream, in this continuous replenishing of life force, experiencing the Wheel of the Year as a microcosm, as darkness begins to replace the sun's light.

Reference

"Look Up a Symbol." Sabian Symbols by Lynda Hill. Accessed August 21, 2020. https://sabiansymbols.com/symbol-lookup/.

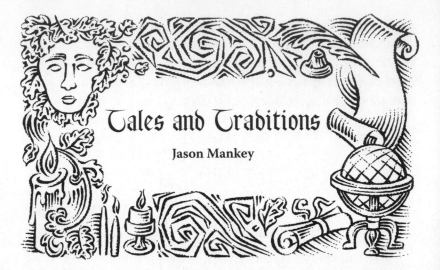

Tales and Traditions

Jason Mankey

WHEN I LIVED IN Michigan, visiting the local apple orchard was like an annual pilgrimage. Sometime after the first frost in September we'd head out to spend a day among the apple trees. Michigan is home to a variety of apples, and we'd stock up on several varieties—some for just eating and others for pies. No trip to the orchard was complete without stopping to see the fresh (non-alcoholic, non-filtered) cider being made, and of course we had to drink some as well.

Mabon: Gather Round the Apple Tree

Apple trees can be found worldwide but were first cultivated in central Asia from a wild ancestor. Today there are over seven thousand different varieties of apples, though most grocery stores only carry a handful of varietals. Throw ten apple seeds into a pot and the resulting trees will produce ten different kinds of apples, most of them inedible. Because of this most of the apples we eat today are the result of trees that have been grafted together. Grafting involves joining the rootstock of a young apple tree onto a living branch from an established variety. The end result will be a tree that produces the fruit from the branch that was added to the rootstock.

Even with the popularity of grafting, apples continue to be grown from seeds; it's how we find new varietals! During America's westward expansion, settlers were required by law to grow apple (or pear) trees on their property. Figures like the legendary Johnny Appleseed cultivated small apple orchards grown from seeds on the outside edge of westward expansion and would then sell their baby trees to settlers so those pioneers could meet the "grow an orchard of fifty trees" requirement (Means 2011, 88). Even though most of the apples that resulted from these orchards were not fit for eating, the resulting fruit would be turned into (hard) cider and "applejack" a type of highly alcoholic brandy. It was thought that a settler who could produce their own booze would be a settler likely to stay for a while.

Apples show up in both mythology and folktales. Most of us are familiar with the evil queen who poisons Snow White with a venomous apple that causes near eternal slumber, but not every story involving the apple is negative. The apple is often portrayed as the fruit produced by the "tree of knowledge," which is then eaten by Eve and Adam in the Bible's Garden of Eden. Eating that apple gets the biblical pair kicked out of Eden but gives them the ability to discern good from evil. In most monotheistic traditions this is seen as a negative, but Christian Gnostics viewed the eating of the apple as essential for awakening humanity's collective consciousness.

The famous Trojan War is the result of a particularly beautiful, or perhaps cursed, apple. Upset at not being invited to a wedding feast, the goddess Eris tossed a golden apple into the party inscribed with the words "for the most beautiful." This apple of discord sparked an argument between Aphrodite, Athena, and Hera over just who was the most beautiful and could thus claim the apple. Too wise to make such a judgement himself, the god Zeus appointed the city of Troy's Prince Paris to render a decision on the most beautiful goddess. Paris chose Aphrodite, and she rewarded Paris with the love of Helen (the most beautiful mortal woman in the world), who was already married to King Menelaus of Sparta, thus sparking the hostilities between Greece and Troy.

In Norse mythology, the goddess Iðunn (also spelled Idunn and Ydun) was the goddess of apples and eternal youth. Iðunn guarded and cultivated the apples that kept the Norse gods forever young. Not surprisingly, the other gods were very protective of her. It's possible that in some way it's Iðunn who inspired the popular phrase "an apple a day keeps the doctor away."

The most famous apple goddess is probably Pomona, the Roman goddess of orchards and fruit. Pomona's name literally means "fruit" and comes from the Latin word for fruit, *pōmus*. In French the apple is still linked directly to Pomona, where it's known as a *pomme* (one of the few words I remember from high school French class). Pomona's feast day was November 1, just after Samhain, which may be why apples are still a part of many Samhain and fall gatherings.

Apples are often associated with divination, especially in the fall when they are most abundant. In Great Britain it was believed that slicing and eating an apple at midnight on Halloween would result in the image of a future lover appearing in a mirror. Similar traditions suggest sleeping with an apple under a pillow in order to see a future love in a dream; the apple was then eaten in the morning to make the dream come true. Fall games such as bobbing for apples began as a form of divination. In the original Scottish version, a bobber who ended up with a mouthful of apple was destined to be wed within a year.

Believing that no part of an apple should go to waste, even the seeds (called "pips") were used for divination. Dropping the pips into a fire while saying the names of potential love interests was said to reveal who one should pursue romantically. If one of the seeds "popped" while a particular name was said, the named individual was thought to be "the one."

In England, apple trees were so important that they were annually "wassailed" during the (Yuletide) holiday season. Usually occurring just after Christmas, the wassailers would sing songs and give offerings to their apple and pear trees to ensure their continued vitality. Wassailing the trees was also thought to drive bad spirits away from the orchards. Because Yuletide can be overly busy, this is a custom that can be easily adapted and done in the fall and doesn't even require that you visit an apple tree. All that it requires are sincere words of thanks to your local apple trees, and a gift of some kind, generally alcoholic and including apples.

Perhaps my favorite way to celebrate with apples in the fall is to serve them during rituals and proclaim them "the Witch's fruit." The most common symbol of Witchcraft, the pentagram (a five-pointed star) is naturally a part of most apples. Cut an apple in half at its middle (the "top" of the apple being the stem) and you'll reveal the pentagram for all to see. For this reason, and dozens of others, apples and their goddesses are popular with Witches and Pagans every autumn. Hail the apple!

References

Boyer, Corinne. *Under the Witching Tree*. London: Troy Books, 2016.

Mankey, Jason. *Llewellyn's Little Book of Yule*. Woodbury MN: Llewellyn Publications, 2020.

Means, Howard. *Johnny Appleseed: The Man, The Myth, the American Story*. New York: Simon and Schuster, 2011.

Skal, David, J. *Death Makes a Holiday: A Cultural History of Halloween*. New York: Bloomsbury Books, 2002.

Feasts and Treats

Elizabeth Barrette

MABON IS THE FALL equinox, when light and dark hang in balance. It's a rustic holiday, and it finds echoes in many harvest festivals around the world. The bounties of field and forest are brought in to stock against the long winter.

Hazelnut Salmon Fillets

Legend says that the Salmon of Wisdom feasted on the hazelnuts that fell into its sacred pool, and thus eating the salmon conveyed all of that wisdom. This quick, simple dish combines those two ingredients, creating a sweet crust of hazelnut crumbs over tender, flaky fish.

Prep time: 5 minutes
Cooking time: 5–6 minutes
Servings: 6

sea salt
black pepper
12 hazelnuts
6 salmon fillets

Sprinkle sea salt and black pepper lightly over the salmon fillets.
Grind 12 hazelnuts in a mortar and pestle or spice grinder to produce a coarse meal. Distribute the hazelnut meal over the salmon fillets.

If you have a folding grill, simply heat it up, put the salmon inside, and cook for 5 minutes. If using a charcoal grill, you will need to flip the fillets; cook for 2–3 minutes per side.

Spiced Nuts

Many edible nuts and seeds ripen at this time of year. While delicious fresh, they taste even better when roasted and seasoned. Warming spices and salty ingredients make this recipe ideal for cool weather.

Prep time: 20 minutes
Cooking time: 5 minutes, plus 12–15 minutes
Servings: 16

olive oil cooking spray
1 cup almonds
½ cup peanuts
½ cup macadamia nuts
½ cup Brazil nuts
¼ cup cashews
¼ cup walnut halves
¼ cup hazelnuts
¼ cup pine nuts
2 tablespoons pistachios
2 tablespoons pepitas (pumpkin seeds)
2 tablespoons sunflower seeds
2 tablespoons sesame seeds
1 teaspoon cumin seeds
1 teaspoon coriander seeds
½ teaspoon green peppercorns
½ teaspoon grains of paradise
1 teaspoon ginger

¼ teaspoon cayenne

6 tablespoons unsalted butter (Margarine won't set, and you will be left with nuts swimming in spicy syrup.)

¼ cup brown sugar, firmly packed

1 teaspoon sea salt

1 teaspoon spirulina

(For a nut-free version, simply replace those with equivalent or slightly smaller quantities of seeds.)

Preheat the oven to 375°F. Line a rimmed baking sheet with aluminum foil and spray it with olive oil or another cooking spray.

For this recipe, you need unsalted nuts and seeds removed from their shells, as you will be adding salt later. Measure out the nuts and seeds one type at a time, examining them to make sure there are no hard shells or other debris. For those that have a papery husk around them, gently rub with a clean cotton dishcloth to remove any loose husks. Otherwise, the spice mixture will adhere to the husks instead of the nuts themselves.

In a large bowl, combine 1 cup almonds, ½ cup peanuts, ½ cup macadamia nuts, ½ cup Brazil nuts, ¼ cup cashews, ¼ cup walnut halves, ¼ cup hazelnuts, ¼ cup pine nuts, 2 tablespoons pistachios, 2 tablespoons pepitas (pumpkin seeds), 2 tablespoons sunflower seeds, and 2 tablespoons sesame seeds. Stir gently to mix them together.

In a small nonstick skillet, combine 1 teaspoon cumin seeds, 1 teaspoon coriander seeds, ½ teaspoon green peppercorns, and ½ teaspoon grains of paradise. Toast them carefully over low heat, stirring constantly, until they just begin to darken in color and grow more fragrant. Pour them out of the skillet into a small bowl and let them cool. Then grind them with a mortar and pestle or spice grinder. Pour the ground spices back into the small bowl.

To the small bowl of ground spices, add 1 teaspoon ginger and ¼ teaspoon cayenne. Stir to combine all the spices evenly.

In a small nonstick skillet, put ⅜ cup unsalted butter and heat until melted. Add ¼ cup of firmly packed brown sugar. Stir gently until the sugar melts into the butter.

Pour the ground spice mixture into the skillet of melted butter and whisk everything together. Make sure there are no lumps to avoid an excessive concentration of spices.

Add the sea salt and the spirulina to the melted butter ¼ teaspoon at a time, alternating the two salty ingredients. Taste as you go, until the spiced butter is as salty as you want it. (Remember that both the salt and the spices will get diluted as they spread across the nuts later.) Typically you will need about 1 teaspoon of sea salt and 1 teaspoon of spirulina to flavor the 4 cups of assorted nuts and seeds.

Pour the spiced butter over the mixed nuts. Stir gently until all of the nuts are coated with spiced butter.

Scrape the spiced nuts onto the rimmed baking sheet and spread them out. It's okay if the tiny seeds stick to the big nuts, but try to keep the big nuts from touching each other. (If the baking sheet is small, you may need to cook them in batches.) Bake the spiced nuts at 375°F, stirring every 5 minutes until they turn golden and fragrant. It typically takes 12–15 minutes.

Remove the pan and set it on a rack to cool. The nuts will be hot and sticky at first. As soon as they cool enough to eat safely, taste-test them. As long as they remain sticky, you can still adjust the flavor by sprinkling and stirring. Eventually they will dry out and be ready to eat.

The exact serving size of nuts and seeds varies by type, but ¼ cup is a good serving size for mixed nuts. By that measure, this recipe makes 16 servings. A lovely way to present spiced nuts is to buy cupcake liners in Mabon colors or themes, like autumn leaves. A standard cupcake liner will comfortably hold ¼ cup of spiced nuts.

Corn and Bean Salad

In the harvest season, many grains and legumes ripen. A few summer vegetables remain. The corn and beans combine to make this a hearty side dish or a vegetarian main dish. Fresh tomatoes and green onions brighten the flavor.

Prep time: 15 minutes
Servings: 12

1 can (15 ounces) yellow kernel corn
1 can (15 ounces) white kernel corn
1 can (15 ounces) black beans
1 can (15 ounces) white navy beans
2 large tomatoes, diced
1 bunch green onions (about 1 cup chopped)
4 tablespoons maple vinegar
4 tablespoons maple syrup
4 tablespoons sunflower oil
1 tablespoon lime juice
½ teaspoon sea salt
¼ teaspoon ground cumin
¼ teaspoon smoked paprika
¼ teaspoon black pepper
¼ teaspoon white pepper
½ cup fresh cilantro, chopped

Open 1 can yellow kernel corn and 1 can white kernel corn. Drain them and pour the corn kernels into a large bowl.

Open 1 can black beans and 1 can white navy beans. Rinse the beans, drain them, and add them to the bowl.

Wash 2 large tomatoes and dice them to bean size. Add them to the bowl. Wash 1 bunch green onions and chop them to bean size (about 1 cup). Add them to the bowl. Stir gently to combine.

In a small bowl, whisk together 4 tablespoons maple vinegar, 4 tablespoons maple syrup, 4 tablespoons sunflower oil, and 1 tablespoon lime juice until smooth and creamy.

To the small bowl, add ½ teaspoon sea salt, ¼ teaspoon ground cumin, ¼ teaspoon smoked paprika, ¼ teaspoon black pepper, and ¼ teaspoon white pepper. Whisk to combine.

Pour the dressing over the corn and bean salad. Gently stir the salad until everything is coated. Snip fresh cilantro to make a generous topping (about ½ cup).

Crafty Crafts

Charlie Rainbow Wolf

THIS IS MY FAVORITE time of year, but that could be because it marks the anniversary of my birth! I have fond memories of back-to-school, of seeing the fields ablaze as the farmers burned off their stubble, of bellringing tours and harvest celebrations and folk music with its morris dancers. Although Mabon and the gathering has been celebrated for eons, naming the harvest festival after the Welsh god of the same name is a relatively new occurrence.

Mabon is a time of balance, when the day and the night are of equal length. Even though this is a beautiful harmony, the equilibrium is precarious, and with every passing day, the night and the darkness start to take dominion. It's the time of year when I'm scrabbling to get the last of the fruits preserved for the winter and when I leave what my friends and family call my "clay season" and move into my "knitting season."

Simple Knit Shawl

First, I do want to comment that this is not knitting 101. The best way to learn to knit is by watching someone do it and copying their movements. Basic knit and purl stitches are the only ones needed for this project. There are plenty of free online tutorials to teach these. This is a beginner-level pattern, and it is designed for those who have the basic skills and want to start something at Mabon to keep warm through the winter. If enough yarn (about 400 yards) was created from the spindle spinning, use it; it's a great way to bring the energy of the earlier festivals into this one.

Materials

Yarn: I'm a bit of a yarn snob and I do recommend natural fibers, but if only a hand-me-down skein of acrylic is available, use it; there's nothing wrong with this, and some people even prefer it. To me, natural fibers seem to handle differently, and I find them more soothing—and frequently warmer—to wear. They also break down in the ecosystem more efficiently than their manmade counterparts. At least 400 yards is required, more if a longer or wider shawl is being constructed, and if this is your first time knitting, choose a plied yarn—more than one strand spun together, it will be more robust and split less—and a medium weight, somewhere around category 5 is ideal. As the yarn is selected, think about the colors of Mabon; harvest colors of brick red, mustard yellow, or olive green are appropriate. As a beginner's knitting project, I'd suggest staying away from the variegated yarn and choosing a solid color; it's easier to see the stitches that way.

Knitting needles: The thickness of the needles will depend on the thickness of the yarn. For a category 5 yarn, choose 5 mm knitting needles; it makes it easier to remember that way! There are all styles available. I like the straight needles as that is how I learned, but many of my friends prefer circular needles. It matters not which are chosen; this project is knitted back and forth, not in the round.

Scissors and a large-eye needle: This is fairly self explanatory; the scissors are to cut remnants of yarn and the large eye needle is for weaving in the ends left when casting on, casting off, or joining a fresh ball of yarn.

Cost: A good 200-yard ball of worsted medium weight wool can be obtained for $7–$10; and to get 400 yards two would be required, making the total cost under $20. Man-made equivalents are maybe $4, or $8 for two. Basic knitting needles can be found for under $5. Large-eye needles (sometimes called tapestry needles) are sold in packets for $3–$5.

Time spent: How fast do you knit? When I was recovering from my broken humerus, I used knitting as physical therapy and was knocking out two of these shawls a week. Your mileage is going to vary depending on your skill level and the spare time you have to devote to completing the project.

Cast Away!

The knitting pattern is designed to be a multiple of four; one for each season—or each corner of the globe or each point of the compass. In numerology, the number 4 is grounded, secure, stable. I'm sharing the basic pattern for medium weight yarn; if the yarn is thicker, cast on less stitches, and if it is finer, cast on more. Remember, multiple of four, always.

Cast on 60 stitches. Use the method you're most comfortable with. I favour the cable cast on method; it makes a neat edge.

Every row is as follows:

Slip the first stitch purlwise from the lefthand needle to the righthand needle.

Knit three, purl 1 until the last four stitches, then knit four.

That's it! This pattern produces a fully reversible fabric with a distinctive ribbed pattern. Keep going until the shawl is the desired length. I find six feet works well, but it's all a matter of personal choice. When you are finished, weave in the ends.

Before the shawl is worn, it needs to be blocked. Lay it on a flat surface and gently mist it with water—I use an old spray bottle. While it is damp, gently stretch it, so that the stitch pattern opens up. Leave it to dry naturally.

There's a wonderful urban legend about the different knitting patterns on the British fishermen's ganseys being their identity should they get washed ashore. Many families did have their own designs, but the bit about them being washed ashore is rather fanciful. What is fact, though, is when you've knit your own garment, you've not just made something of warmth and beauty. You've aligned your creative frequency with one that is many centuries old and manifested the energies of your ancestors.

Further Reading

Teach Yourself To Knit (Leisure Arts #623) by Evie Rosen and Leisure Arts, 1988.

Patons Woolcraft (#17534): The Basic Guide to Knitting & Crochet from First Steps to Finishing Touches by Coats and Patons, 1988.

Knitting 101: Master Basic Skills and Techniques Easily through Step-by-Step Instruction by Carri Hammett, 2012.

Online Resources

Because it is often easier to do something by copying than by reading about it, I highly recommend you check out Wool and the Gang's videos on YouTube. They're very well presented and easy to follow.

"How to Do a Cable Cast-On" by Wool and the Gang

"How to Knit" by Wool and the Gang

"How to Knit: Purl Stitch" by Wool and the Gang

"How to Cast off Your Knitting" by Wool and the Gang

Reference

White, Sarah E. "How to Do a Cable Cast on When Knitting." The Spruce Crafts. Dotdash. Updated May 14, 2020, https://www.thesprucecrafts.com/how-to-do-cable-cast-on-2116502.

Candle Magic

Ember Grant

AT AUTUMN, HARVEST SEASON is in full swing, and we typically associate harvest with abundance, which can include wealth and success. At this time of year, day and night are equal in length, making it a good time for spells of balance. This is also a transitional time as daylight wanes and we approach the dark half of the year.

Seven Day Spell for Success

Fire represents strength of will and transformation; it has an authoritative energy, and it can be just the element you need to boost success in any aspect of your life. You can perform this spell for general success, but it works best if you focus on something specific.

You'll need a fairly large candle—a 3 x 6 pillar works best—in orange or yellow. You'll also need a heat-proof plate or platter to burn it on. Anoint the candle as desired—bergamot oil is a good choice.

In addition, you will need some crystals and plant materials for this spell. Choose six different items—a combination of stones and plants. You will start with just the candle and add one item to your altar each day when you relight the candle. The plant materials can be fresh or dried, but keep in mind if they're fresh and you use them early in the week, they will be sitting around for seven days.

• These crystals are associated with the element of fire and with success: ruby, garnet, jasper, aqua aura quartz, citrine, diamond, gold, malachite, tiger's-eye.

• Oak is associated with the sun and the fire element and has been revered by many cultures throughout history. Any part of the tree can be used—bark, wood, leaf, branch or twig, or acorn. It is often used in spells for luck, prosperity, and protection.

• Orange is associated with the sun and fire, luck, and prosperity.

• Pomegranate also has a history of being used for good fortune; it's associated with fire and Mercury, and is used for wishes.

• Holly also has a history of bringing good fortune, and it's associated with fire and Mars.

• Star anise can usually be found in the spice section of the supermarket. It's associated with air and Jupiter but is also used to draw good luck.

• Sunflower is associated with the sun and fire and with granting wishes.

• Basil and clove are associated with wealth.

• Cinnamon and ginger are associated with success; you can sprinkle these in ground form or use cinnamon in stick form and fresh or dried ginger.

Over the course of the week, approach this like you're stoking a fire, adding more fuel and building it up. Simply place the items on the plate around the base of the candle. It doesn't matter which component you add on which day, just that you add something new and continue lighting the candle. Try to work during a waxing moon phase, with the last day of the spell being a full moon.

As you light the candle each day, say these words:

Day one—*The start, the spark to be my best. I set foundation for success.*

Day two—*Like fuel to fire, I keep reaching higher.*

Day three—*Burning hotter, burning longer, my will is getting stronger.*

Day four—*It may take time, but success will be mine.*

Day five—*The power of this flame will help me reach my aim.*

Day six—*Success is near, the way is clear.*

Day seven—*Feel the heat, success is sweet!*

Let the candle burn for an hour each day on the first two days, then two hours each day for the following days. If it's a very large candle, like a three-wick, you can let it burn longer each day if you wish.

On the last day, let the candle burn as long as you wish; if it's small enough, allow it to burn out. If not, keep relighting it each day until it's done, then dispose of it. Keep the stones and herbs on your altar as long as you like or make a bundle of them to carry with you. When you feel ready, cleanse the stones and bury the plant materials.

Fruit and Fire: A Spell for Healing

The apple appears often in fairy tales, legends, and myths from around the world and is often associated with knowledge, wisdom, immortality, temptation, good fortune, abundance, and love. They are reputed to have healing properties as well, and we all know they're nutritious. Metaphysically, apples are associated with the planet Venus and the element of water. Apples actually originated in Kazakhstan and are members of the rose (*Rosaceae*) family. And, of course, the five seeds inside form a star pattern within a circle—a pentacle—another reason they're often associated with magic.

Because apples are extra popular this time of year, we'll use them in this candle spell for healing. You can focus on general well-being or, if necessary, something specific you need help with.

Slice a large apple horizontally in five thin slices and arrange these on a heat-proof plate. Put one in the center and four on the edges, or arrange them in a star shape. Place a white tea light candle on each slice.

As you light the candles, visualize your healing goals. Imagine the candle flames burning away any illness or negativity and charging your body with wellness and healing energy. When all the candles are burning, sit before the plate for as long as you like and continue to meditate on healing. Whisper this chant as many times as you desire:

Fruit and fire, sweet and bright, fill me with your healing light.

Allow the candles to burn out. You can dry the apple slices if you wish and use them in potpourri or other crafts, or bury them. Eat or discard the rest of the apple.

Mabon Ritual

Kate Freuler

THE NIGHT OF THE fall equinox is perfect for saying goodbye to situations, attachments, or anything that has run its course, just like the summer is. Endings aren't always bad. Any tarot reader will tell you that pulling the death card doesn't herald a tragedy or physical death, but rather a new beginning. One thing must end in order for something new to begin, so death and rebirth are one and the same. For this reason, it makes sense that endings can, in fact, be embraced and viewed as hopeful and positive. Just as we appreciate the sun as it recedes, we can also see the beauty in the things we choose to release.

The Beauty of Endings

This Mabon ritual can be done alone or as a group during sunset on the equinox. It centers on a dying leaf, which should be chosen with intention. Find the prettiest one you can, with the brightest colors and most striking patterns. The purpose of choosing a leaf that has become colorful and unique in its death is to signify that endings can be beautiful and cherished. Even difficult things can be appreciated for the lessons they've brought.

In this ritual, you'll name things in your life that you'd like to put to rest or let "die," so to speak, in order to make room for new growth. To help focus these intentions, we'll be using the elements to identify different areas of release. Below is a description of each element and the life experiences that can be associated with them. Using this information, choose four issues in your own life—one for each element—that you'd like to let go of. It might help to write these down for later.

Earth: The physical body and surroundings. Earth represents all material and physical situations. Some examples of earth-ruled things you might want to banish are financial insecurity, physical health problems, and job issues.

Air: The mind and intellect. Air encompasses communication and learning. Some examples of things associated with air you might wish to move on from are unresolved disagreements, obsessions, and mental or creative blockages.

Fire: The spirit and passion. Fire is the realm of zeal and fervour. You might associate fire with letting go of anger issues, grudges, or impulsive behaviour.

Water: Emotion and empathy. Water is the realm of deep feeling. Things associated with water that you might want to lay to rest are melancholy, anxiety, ill-placed love, or codependency.

Supplies:
A dying leaf
A bowl of water
A dish of ashes from a fire or incense
A stone
A feather
Access to an outdoor area
A large bowl if you're indoors

Gather your materials in a secluded, private space. Cast a circle if you wish. Stand facing the west and say:

On this night I say goodbye to the sun as I welcome the darkness.
I face the coming cold with strength.
I embrace change with courage.
I acknowledge the beauty of that which is passing.

Spend a moment in silence, noticing the transition of day to night as dusk falls upon you. Feel the darkness descending over the land, the shadows lengthening and filling every corner. Sense the chill of the air against your skin and breathe deep the smell of autumn.

If you're outdoors, make a shallow hole in the ground and place the leaf in it. If you're indoors, place it in a bowl. Say:

As the sun recedes, I let go of that which has run its course. I acknowledge and respect what the universe has taught me and lovingly let it go. As this leaf rots and decays, it will transform into new life, as will the things that I shed on this night.

Hold the feather up toward the east. Bearing in mind the issues you associated with air beforehand, state that which you're letting go of and why you're thankful for it. Some examples: "I release my shyness. I'm thankful to have learned the value of my own voice." Or, "I release all lingering conflict and have learned the value of standing up for myself."

After stating your intentions, say:

This feather holds the energy of my experience. I give it over to the darkness.

Place the feather upon the leaf.

Moving counterclockwise, face the north and hold the stone toward the sky. State your earth-related intentions out loud. Some examples: "I release my overspending habits and am thankful to have learned to enjoy intangible things." Or, "I release the job I've out-grown and am thankful for the chance to find a better path."

After stating your intentions, say:

This stone holds the energy of my experience. I give it over to the darkness.

Place the stone upon the leaf.

Next, face the west, holding the bowl of water to the sky. State your water-related intentions. For example: "I release my excessive worry over the opinions of others and am thankful for the peace that takes its place." Or, "I release my emotional attachment to (person) and have learned the value of independence."

After stating your intentions, say:

This water holds the energy of my experience. I give it over to the darkness.

Pour the water over the leaf.

Last, turn to the south and hold the dish of ashes up to the sky, stating your fire-related intention. For example: "I release my irritability over things I can't control and from this I've learned patience." Or, "I release my anger over past events and am thankful to have learned the importance of walking away."

After stating your intentions, say:

These ashes hold the energy of my experience. I give it over to the darkness.

Dump the ashes on the leaf.

Now stand before the gathered objects and say:

As night falls, I lay the past to rest in the earth, to decay, reform, and fertilize the future. I am now set free to transform.

If you're indoors, now is the time to go outside to a private place. Dig a shallow hole in the ground and pour the contents of the bowl (leaf, ashes, water, and feather) into the shallow grave.

Pull the earth over top of the leaf and other objects, covering them completely. State:

I lay the past to rest, deep in the dark of transformation.

Walk away from the "grave" as night falls, leaving the past behind.

Notes for Performing This Ritual as a Group

This ritual is suitable for any number of people with some minor tweaking. For the speaking parts of this working, select a person ahead of time to recite the words and change the word "I" to "we." During the ritual, have the group stand in a circle around the leaf. Pass each of the elemental objects around the circle counterclockwise allowing each participant to state their intentions for each. When everyone has done so, place the object on the leaf. At the end, each person can place a handful of dirt on the grave before walking away.

Notes

Notes

Notes

Notes

Notes

Notes

Notes